The Shared Pulpit

A Sermon Seminar for Lay People

Erika Hewitt

Skinner House Books
Boston

www.skinnerhouse.org

Printed in the United States

Cover and text design by Suzanne Morgan
Front cover photo of the sanctuary of First Church in Jamaica Plain, Unitarian Universalist, by Jennifer Waddell, www.jenniferwaddellphotography.com

print ISBN: 978-1-55896-722-9
eBook ISBN: 978-1-55896-728-1

6 5 4 3 2 1
15 14

Library of Congress Cataloging-in-Publication Data

Hewitt, Erika A.
   The shared pulpit : a sermon seminar for lay people / Erika Hewitt.
      pages cm
   Includes bibliographical references.
   ISBN 978-1-55896-722-9 (pbk. : alk. paper) 1. Lay preaching—Study and teaching. 2. Laity—Unitarian Universalist Association. I. Title.
   BV4235.L3H49 2014
   251.0088'2891—dc23
                                        2013032805

We gratefully acknowledge permission to reprint the following: "Shared Ministry: The Language of Listening" by Rev. Jan Carlsson-Bull, by permission of author; "Can't We Get Along? Loving Your Political Opponent" by Rev. Jessica Purple Rodela, by permission of author; Rev. Dr. Patrick T. O'Neill, currently serving as Minister of Rosslyn Hill Unitarian Chapel in London, UK, by permission of author; "Tips for Giving a Truly Terrible Sermon (50 Ways to Lose Your Listeners)" by Rev. Jane Rzepka and Rev. Ken Sawyer, by permission of authors; and Thomas John Carlisle, "Our Jeopardy", *Theology Today* Vol. 43, No. 4, pp. 559, copyright © 1987 by Princeton Theological Seminary, reprinted by permission of SAGE.

Contents

Introduction

Using a series of small group meetings, this program aims to deepen connection and trust among you—the seeking minds and caring hearts of your Unitarian Universalist congregation. It contains advice, tools, and a process designed to equip you to be even more skilled, confident leaders (because anyone brave and curious enough to share their journey publicly with their congregation is, in fact, a leader). Along the way, you'll discover your authentic voice by writing a sermon to deliver to the congregation.

This program has been pulpit-and-pew tested, producing dozens of graduates who report that it transformed their relationship to their congregation and to Unitarian Universalism. As a participant, you don't need to think of yourself as a writer. You don't have to know what you want to say. You don't even need to be a visible leader in your congregation. As you and five to seven others navigate your way through the eight sessions presented here—under the guidance of a group leader—you have to do only three things:

- commit your time and energy to the program—including doing the required writing between sessions
- create and uphold a group covenant so that those in your group can risk being vulnerable
- trust that the first two steps will reveal your voice and your truth.

A note about language: In some UU congregations, people regularly and comfortably use words like *sermon*, *preach*, and *worship*. Some Unitarian Universalists, however, may use the word *preaching* only when referring to the congregation's ordained minister delivering sermons. In other congregations, members may avoid these words altogether. This book uses these words and invites you to explore the many layers of their meanings. It assumes that our congregations are enriched when members make this exploration part of their "responsible search for truth and meaning"—a process that sometimes entails redefining and reclaiming emotionally charged words.

Anyone—and Everyone—Can Minister

In our Unitarian Universalist tradition, we speak of shared ministry—the embodied belief that everyone, not just the ordained minister, takes part in the ministry of the congregation. In other words, anyone can minister. Sometimes those who minister most tenderly are those from whom we least expect it and those who hardly expect it of themselves.

To minister literally means "to serve" (from the Latin *ministrare*): to serve the needs of others—a rather pale definition, given its numerous forms. But ministry is less about what we do and more about who we are. We minister by who we are as people, not by our titles. So it is with laypeople: Ministry comes from being authentically *you*. In the words of Rev. Beth Graham, "Who each of us is in this world is the gift we bring to our mutual ministry."

Here's an illustration of this basic but surprising truth: For over six years, I've been part of the letter-writing ministry operated by our UU Church of the Larger Fellowship. Since then, dozens of letters have travelled between me and my incarcerated pen pal, Olugbala (as he wishes to be named in these pages). I'm embarrassed to say that when I began writing letters to Olugbala, I unwittingly assumed that I would be doing the heavy lifting regarding ministry: that I would be filling his well and giving to him without receiving much in return (except, perhaps, the pats on the back I'd give myself).

How wrong I was. Over the past seven years, the letters that Olugbala and I have exchanged are full of respect, admiration, and genuine affection for one another; he has ministered to me many times. In one letter to Olugbala, I admitted to struggling with a difficult decision. His next letter contained both comfort and wise advice. Over the years, his encouragement has lifted my spirits, his observations have led to new insights, and his friendship has made my life sweeter. Olugbala—an "uneducated" man who's spent his entire adult life behind bars—ministers to me.

All of us can minister. Many of us do, by virtue of who we are in the world and how we enter into relationship with others. There are surely many people in your congregation whose shared ministry can include writing and delivering a sermon.

The Origins of the Program

When I entered parish ministry over a decade ago, I realized that my parishioners have life experiences as compelling as my own and theological beliefs as interesting and important as mine. Our Unitarian Universalist tradition reminds us that within every life there's value, insight, and wisdom worth voicing. After many years of leading this program in my congregation, it's clear to me that many members of our UU congregations are excellent pulpit speakers.

And here's a confession: My somewhat crass motivation in creating this program was to ensure that the eight or so sermons presented by congregation members that year would be solid (read: "not embarrassing should visitors be present"). I quickly realized that I'd set my expectations too low. As the first cadre of Summer Sermon Seminar participants moved through the program, I was gratified to witness the way they bonded with each other. Even after three-hour sessions, they huddled in twos and threes at the end of the evening, gently touching shoulders as they asked deeper questions. They sought each other out on Sunday mornings, eager to resume the new connections they'd forged.

Then, another delightful surprise. As the program unfolded, inviting longer and longer reflections from each person, I was astonished to observe how quickly they grew into graceful and poised speakers, and how meaningful their sermons became. By combing through their life experiences and sharing stories "passed through the fire" of spiritual reflection, all participants blossomed into confident lay preachers I watched as they grew a confident, quiet authority in their own spiritual lives. They testified that the program filled their need for meaning.

The final surprise was the profound connecting effect when a participant delivered their sermon to the congregation. Once they wrote their truth and preached their wisdom, it was as if they'd shared a piece of their soul with their beloved community—and the community saw them in a new light. No other program so intensely transformed the congregation's life. Spiritual growth is at once the medium and the message of the program.

As I've continued to shape this program, I do so as a person of faith wrestling with what it means to find my own voice and speak my own truth. This is a small group spiritual development program, not The Gospel according to Me! Many of our congregations can benefit from a program like this: It offers both the functional advantage of providing engaging sermons by laypeople and the spiritual gift of creating intimacy as their wisdom and connective power unfolds. At the heart of this program is the steadfast belief that strong is what we make each other.

Leading the Program

A good leader is essential, although this program can be led by a professional minister or a lay leader. For a variety of reasons, it's important that a single person facilitate this program rather than sharing the leadership among group members.

In one sense, the leader's responsibilities are logistical: gathering the supplies and acting as timekeeper for each session. The deeper layer of responsibility, however, resembles that of a worship leader during worship: to create a container in which participants can bring their best selves, take risks, and connect with each other. To paraphrase Antoine de Saint-Exupéry: When building a ship, a good leader will drum up people to collect wood and will assign them tasks, as well as teach them to long for the endless immensity of the sea. The Leader's Notes section contains additional general advice for leaders as well as specific recommendations for facilitating each session; it begins on page 83.

How the Program Works

Following this Introduction, "The Worship Vessel" presents the big picture of Unitarian Universalist worship—because approaching a sermon without acknowledging its larger context is like selecting furniture without knowing anything about the space it's for: It helps to know where it's going, and why, to ensure a good fit. The chapter addresses the purposes and possibilities of worship. Invoking the voices of other UU ministers, it also reflects on larger issues of safety, risk, vulnerability, and mistakes as they apply to preaching. Finally, it explores the metaphor of the worship experience as a vessel, a container for spiritual growth.

Each of the eight session plans of the program is presented in an outline format, starting with a snapshot of the session's overall objective. The session plans are accompanied by readings and instructions for your time together, as well as discussion questions. Each session concludes with a list of the pieces to read in preparation for the next gathering—these include sermons that model a particular aspect of the session's focus.

At the start of a session, participants spend about fifteen minutes engaged in silent writing. I dub this Chalice Pages, an adaptation of the process called Morning Pages that Julia Cameron made famous in her book *The Artist's Way: A Spiritual Path to Creativity*. Cameron suggests writing three handwritten pages every day, first thing in the morning, no matter what. She says to just write, even if it's "I don't have anything to write today." No matter what you feel drawn to write, you do it not to produce something but to be alone with the page. Participants in this program are free to explore Chalice Pages in this way—or to do anything else with their fifteen minutes. The three-pages guideline is less important, in this context, than the time. With the exception of two sessions early in the program, no instructions are given for Chalice Pages, other than the request that participants write in silence.

About one minute before the Chalice Pages time ends, the group leader silently lights the chalice. This signals that it's time to finish any last thoughts before the group transitions into active listening and responding. At the end of the session, the Chalice Pages forms a similar threshold for people to land back in their lives, providing an opportunity for participants to process what they've heard over the course of the evening or jot down thoughts they don't want to lose. After about fourteen minutes of silent writing, the group leader extinguishes the chalice, signaling that it's time to pack up to go. Many participants (especially introverts) find that the ritual of starting and ending each session with silent reflection is powerful and transformative. At the very least, it allows people to arrive and leave in a gentle way.

The program is shaped around two distinct but important steps: taking the raw material of our life stories and refining it through the process of theological reflection. The heart of this process is the work that you, the participants, will bring: your writing, putting pen to paper (or fingers to keyboard) in order to invite your authentic voice to emerge. Therefore, preparing for each session involves writing reflections, the length of which slowly increases with each session, morphing into a sermon by the final gatherings. At times, these reflections are guided by suggestions or instructions from the previous session. The reflection topics can change from session to session, or participants can stick to the same one, reworking it over and over. (Sermons are created for the voice and the ears, so it's counter to the spirit of the program to distribute written copies of one's reflection.) The listening itself is meant to be a spiritual, not editorial, exercise. When a participant is done reading their reflection, the group sits in silence for a minute to provide a space that allows the reflection to filter down from the head to the heart. The group's listening and offering of feedback is also guided by a covenant, developed by the group members according to their needs.

Due to this investment of time and heart, the program is designed to last for eight sessions, not eight weeks. It's most effective to spread the sessions two or three weeks apart. Over the course of the program, the content of the group's work shifts slightly. In the first half of the program, each session includes time to discuss various aspects of worship or preaching theory. These discussions help shape the writing and reflections. In addition, some of the provided readings encourage participants to think about how the realms of writing and preaching intersect.

Summary of the Sessions

Here's a quick outline of the focus of each session:

Session 1: Getting to know each other; what makes a sermon and what it means to have "authority" in the pulpit. Guiding question: What do you have to say that no one else can say?

Session 2: Your group covenant; finding your voice and telling your story; how to choose a topic and structure stories. Guiding question: What does your voice sound like?

Session 3: Worship nuts and bolts. Guiding questions: What freedom and creativity remain within the limits of rules? What images or metaphors appear in your reflections?

Session 4: Moving away from story-telling to thinking theologically; the process of theological reflection. Guiding question: How have my experiences and my stories shaped my spirituality?

Session 5: Going deeper; reading and listening. Guiding questions: How do our stories turn into theological reflection?

Session 6: Polishing. Guiding question: What have you discovered in yourself and in one another?

Sessions 7 and 8: Listening to sermons. Guiding question: What image or metaphor might your worship service center around? As you build a worship service around your sermon, how can worship elements complement and strengthen your sermon's image or metaphor?

The Worship Vessel

In our Unitarian Universalist tradition, what is required of those who prepare and deliver sermons? What does it mean to offer wisdom and hope to members of a gathered community?

These are great responsibilities. Each worship service is a unique moment in a congregation's life. Not every member of the congregation will be present at any particular service—that would be a hard feat. Gathering for an hour on Sunday, though, is a physical reminder of the community we've chosen to call home. Worship is both a calling forth of our best selves and an expression of acceptance of people as they are. It's a vessel in which we meet one another, again and again, to remind ourselves of who we are and who we wish to be. As a core component of worship, the sermon is an essential piece of our worship life—whether it reflects hard-won wisdom, a summons to justice, or the love we can't seem to find within ourselves.

The pulpit is a place to honor what Ralph Waldo Emerson called "life passed through the fire of thought." Our message needs to be spoken through the voices of members whose hearts and lives have been changed by Unitarian Universalism. As you make your way through this program, I hope that you discover a new piece of your ministry—which is, after all, way bigger than a fifteen- or twenty-minute sermon. Stirring your gifts to life means that you're growing as a spiritual leader—and that will make your congregation healthier and more spirit-filled.

What Is Worship For?

Worship is a central experience of Unitarian Universalism, serving many purposes and diverse needs. Rarely should worship be used to convey information; your time together in worship is too precious to use as a means to deliver data. Rather, worship is about who we are in relationship to ourselves, each other, and the larger life. As a parish minister, I believe not in a fixed, unnamable God but in That Which Is Larger Than Us. For me, this "Larger Than" force—call it the Cosmos, the Mystery, or the Gathered Community—is at the center of the worship experience. Worship is my favorite part of congregational life precisely for that reason: by devoting ourselves to encountering and engaging That Which Is Greater/Wiser/Stronger/More Compassionate than our individual selves, we place ourselves in a crucible for transformation and healing.

In its most glorious, expansive sense, worship builds up the congregational body for its work in the world—even as we strengthen our relationships with each other, across our many differences. From an institutional standpoint, worship affirms the congregation's power and vision. For the individuals attending—each person carrying a unique set of questions, gladness, longings, and sadness—worship is a wellspring of hope, a container for grief, and a laboratory for meaning-making.

Worship *can* serve all these purposes—but only with the intention and practice of the worship leaders.

Who Is Worship For?

This book assumes that worship is just as much for the newcomer, the visitor, the "shopper," and the seeker as it is for those who created and sustain the congregation. This has far-reaching implications for worship leaders, including preachers.

Worship leaders often gear the service toward the existing community. Familiar patterns and hymns anchor longstanding members in a sense of comfort. Beloved faces greet us, welcome arms encircle us, and we rest in the pleasure of being known by old friends.

However, worship that cements a community's sense of itself often precludes casting a net wide enough to welcome newcomers and seekers. For example, leaders and other may use nicknames and acronyms liberally, even though no visitor or brand-new Unitarian Universalist could be expected to decipher codes like "DRE," "GA," and "youth con." Or in more awkward moments, some worship services can become a stage upon which the drama of personality gets acted out—perhaps through "joys and sorrows" run amok, or worship leaders misinterpreting their primary role as that of entertainer.

When worship services showcase individuals' emotions, experiences, or processes, most of the time the leaders are simply trying to create a sense of familiarity or family among the gathered. It's meant to affirm how finely the web is woven, and to demonstrate publicly how well the congregation knows one another and how deeply we care for one another. However, all too often, these well-intentioned efforts to share the love come across as off-putting—not only to guests but also to those who desperately need a space in which to bring their rawest needs. Worship that celebrates individualism gives the impression, however faulty, that a newcomer must struggle to get into the circle of belonging, and that UU worship is a forum for processing unresolved personal issues.

Who is worship for? Those who already belong? Or those who are hungry to belong and don't know how to find their way in? Is worship solely for those who have anchored their lives in Unitarian Universalism? Or is it also for those looking for a reason to do so?

Holding the Space

All worship leaders—from the minister to musicians to "the sound guy"—share a basic responsibility: to hold the worship space and set the desired tone.

Holding the space can mean many things. I think of worship as a container: a strong, spacious vessel into which each person places themselves and their needs, where they merge with the needs of others. That vessel needs to make room for what people bring with them, and to make a promise about the ways they'll be cared for. When the space is held carefully, there's room for everyone—and then some. When elements of worship are approached in a careless or exclusionary way, however, the vessel tips, sloshing on people's figurative toes.

Setting tone and holding the space aren't necessarily the same thing as creating "safety" in worship. The words *safe* and *safety* are frequently used regarding UU worship and the worship space itself. They deserve some parsing. Many Unitarian Universalist ministers claim that worship isn't supposed to be a safe event so much as a transformational one, a time to be comforted and held even as parishioners are challenged, stretched, and taken outside of their comfortable bubble. (An Episcopal priest I know says of her own Christian tradition, "If we preached the gospel as Jesus had intended, we'd have to install seat belts in the pews.")

The very word *safe*, in fact, is charged for some people, imbued as it is with privilege. Rev. Sean Dennison points out that "the idea of 'safe space' is a cultural construct and the particular culture it comes from is one that has enough privilege to expect and even demand safety. There are so many people in this world who are never completely safe and thus don't expect to be."

For others, safe worship connotes a shallow or self-serving experience. "Far too often, the expectation of worship is a place that simply affirms me and reinforces my worldview," says Rev. Jason Shelton. "While that may be safe in some respects, it's not much of an opportunity for growth. If worship is about transformation, then it's a radically un-safe event."

Two strands of Universalist and Unitarian theology, shaped over centuries of history, explain why worship should focus on transformation.

First, there's what I call The Great Universalist Paradox. This is the double-pronged spiritual legacy of our Universalist ancestors: We believe that every person in the human family is loved; we're all saved; we're all okay just the way we are. And . . . we're not done. Our lives, our very becoming, is unfinished work.

We're Unitarian Universalists today because those who came before us were, as Rev. Kate Braestrup once put it, "cheerfully sure of God's forgiveness for human failure." They were just as certain that the God who holds all people in love isn't done with us yet: the Great and Sanctified Mystery calls us to grow and learn, to serve and liberate others as long as we live. To be a UU is to rest in the faith that we're loved and saved, but ours is a restless resting, as we hunger to engage our growing edges. Our ideal of beloved community constantly rubs up against our flawed humanness.

I believe that UU worship is a playing field on which we wrestle with this delicate, faith-full balance: knowing that we don't need to be any stronger, any wiser, any "better" than we are right now to belong to Life even as we feel compelled to express our gratitude for the gift of life by seeking to grow, learn, and awaken more every day. That transformative process doesn't always feel safe.

Our Unitarian heritage provides a second foundational piece of the puzzle: covenant. Unitarian Universalist worship, along with other aspects of congregational life, is grounded in relationship arising from covenant—the promises a community makes about how they will be with one another. It's not enough to want to live a life of greater integrity; we need help to be the people that we strive to be. Some of us draw encouragement and inspiration from a Larger Presence, from a God whose grace allows us to begin each day anew. Unitarian Universalists also receive this encouragement and strength from each other. This is the transcendent function of community, and therefore of worship: its glorious power to weave our interdependent web more beautifully.

"It's the covenantal community that makes worship safe even when it's challenging, transformational, upsetting, or scary," notes Rev. Mark Glovin. "Our responsibility as worship leaders is to be responsible for the emotional states we create. We can bring people to uncomfortable places but we can't leave them there alone. We have to be there with them, bring them back, wrap up the experience somehow. We have to tread lightly and go to those places with intention."

As a preacher and worship leader, your presence in the pulpit will communicate all of these things. You will help create a "safe enough" space, a place where we take appropriate risks and make ourselves vulnerable even as we challenge one another to grow. You will be a keeper of the vessel of worship, that container at the intersection of reason and mystery that often invites us to the edge—the place where all genuine growth occurs.

Risk and Needs

Worship as a vessel contains The Whole—the whole community as gathered, however full the scope of our needs and individual contexts. When we bring our full selves to worship—with all our joys, all our fears, and the fullness of our life experiences—our differing needs don't fall into perfect alignment. When an aspect of a particular worship service—its topic, its ritual, its music, or its language—doesn't meet our needs, it helps to remember how many different spiritual hungers are borne into the sanctuary every week. If one person isn't being fed, chances are someone else is.

A worship service affords the unique opportunity each week for a congregation's members to define themselves as one strong body, connected by and to a common vision. If one person's particular need goes unmet, it's not that someone else matters more; it's that the whole is being served in a fluid, dynamic dance.

Let this assurance serve as a balm if you're feeling anxious about delivering a sermon to the congregation: By virtue of addressing The Whole, you can't touch every single person. You're not expected to. Your voice and your truth will find the people who long to hear the thing that you have to say. It is enough—and you are enough.

Here's an illustration: When I was a new minister, I decided to experiment with something unusual. Instead of beginning worship with a spoken call to worship as tradition dictated, I led a body prayer for those who chose to participate. The prayer, created by Patricia Mathes Cane and inspired by tai chi practice, is called "the shower of light." I said,

Reach up and bring your hands downward as if receiving a shower of light. Imagine the life force that surrounds you. As you do this movement, notice any stress, tension, or negativity you may be holding and let it go. As you raise your hands again, breathe in the shower of light; as you lower your hands, exhale and let go of any negativity within you. Feel the shower of energy cleansing and renewing you; nourishing your body, mind, and spirit.

Well. Following that service, a church member who was battling cancer reached out to me with gratitude, testifying that he experienced this body prayer as "the most comforting, healing thing." I was heartened: Taking a risk like that hadn't been a mistake; someone had been healed by trying something new. But that same week, another church member came to me with different feedback. "We did that stuff in the sixties," she said, "and we're done with it." The subtext of her message was clear: Stop pushing the envelope because it's just not comfortable for me.

I hadn't expected the body prayer to resonate with everyone. How could it? This story reflects a couple truths. First, some people's needs will go unmet in worship, and those unmet needs can take on a charge. Big feelings carry a big charge. In relationship we carry one another, and sometimes being in right relationship calls us to be tenderly vigilant about how we both name our longing and voice our disappointments.

Second, for better or worse, we're people of the world, and as a consequence, we internalize the seductive messages of our culture that appoint us to be consumers. Sometimes we bring this mentality into worship with us. As consumers, we're accustomed to receiving what we ask for. We expect our needs to be met by the goods and services we seek. How often do we come to church feeling uncomfortable or needy, and expect to be fixed or fulfilled by our worship leaders?

In her blog about worship, Marcia McFee, a United Methodist worship leader, reminds us that each congregation is a diverse body with many needs and preferences:

> Because the Body is inherently diverse (yep, EVERY congregation), there will be times when what we are doing in worship is not necessarily my cup of tea. But all I have to do is just look down the pew or the aisle. There is someone who is being filled in that moment and when one part of the Body is built up, it is good for the whole. And if we have committed to our diversity of expression as a community, I can trust that we will get to "my thing."

A compassionate stance towards UU worship is that everyone involved—choir members, the child lighting the chalice, the preacher (however seasoned)—is doing their best. We worship leaders bring our gifts to the table and ask the community to receive them graciously—not as consumers but as fellow seekers whose hunger for connection or meaning has brought us together.

This is the spirit of this program on creating sermons. When you participate in the seminar, try to do so as a seeker and as someone willing to share your gifts. Whether your group's covenant explicitly states it or not, each of you will be bringing the gift of who you are—along with a dose of admirable courage—to "build up the Body." That is enough. You are enough.

Scorekeeping in Worship

Our Unitarian Universalist congregations strive to see, hear, welcome, and include people who claim theist, humanist, pagan, Christian, Buddhist, agnostic, and many more identities. That's the good news: We try to make room for all beliefs to overlap, finding expression and voice.

The shadow side of this diversity is that at times members feel underrepresented or unacknowledged because of their spiritual beliefs or practices. When a group of parishioners perceives themselves as marginalized or pushed out by the congregation's worship life, their feelings can get hurt, generating uncomfortable conflict.

Believe it or not, conflict over religious diversity isn't necessarily unhealthy. It invites dialogue and is a natural outcome of making room for all—and it's common even in non-UU churches. However, unhealthy conflict emerges when the hurt of one person or group gets expressed as scorekeeping. Here's what worship scorekeeping sounds like:

"We've sung hymns with the word *God* in them for three Sundays in a row."
"Why has it been six months since we heard a humanist sermon?"
"Are the pagans leading worship again? Why do they get to lead worship so often?"

Whether accurate or not, these kinds of questions and comments indicate a deeper emotional divide, implying an "us versus them" mentality. They don't reflect an objective inquiry into how worship might be more effective at building up the Body for its work in the world, and at connecting us to one another across our many differences. (Those inquiries should always be a welcome part of community dialogue.)

If you live with a spouse, partner, or housemate, recall the last time a version of score-keeping occurred in your home. Notice the larger emotional iceberg it was attached to. For example, the statement "It's your turn to take out the trash because I've done it for four weeks straight" isn't really about the trash. Similarly, the person who says, "I've had to pick up your wet towel every day this week" isn't really talking about laundry. Both statements reflect hurts stemming from a perceived imbalance of power or investment in the relationship. They also convey a "digging in" to even the score or restore the imbalance.

In UU congregations, people who engage in worship-related scorekeeping bear the same kind of hurt—the same feeling of being diminished or threatened by theological diversity. Scorekeepers may have lost sight of the larger purpose of worship in particular, and of the covenantal free church in general. Ideally, when we hear language or a story that isn't part of our own religious toolbox, we'd like our response to be, "Wow—as a UU, I love to glimpse the wisdom of paths other than my own." Instead, scorekeeping usually stems from conflict about who's in charge and/or anxiety about "Do I belong?"

As a result, it's not uncommon for someone who feels excluded to volunteer to deliver a sermon or lead worship—not because they feel called to create a fulfilling worship experience but rather to present their issue or perspective so they can be seen, heard, and appreciated. Worship suffers, however, when the motivation behind its creation or implementation is a personal stake rather than a collective commitment. If you recognize a dynamic in your congregation in this description, it doesn't mean that your congregation is damaged or suffers from poor worship (again, conflict is a natural part of being in community). However, it does suggest that larger issues are at play.

Whether you're just considering whether to take part in this program or enthusiastically jumping in with both feet, reflect on your reasons for wanting to participate.

Search your heart, as a gesture of goodwill toward the whole, and remember that, from professional staff to laypeople, worship leaders share a responsibility to the entire worshipping community—not to one group or one interest.

The Theology of Imperfection

Many UU congregations are filled with highly educated, professional, and otherwise successful people whose vocations have required (or invited) them to excel, to achieve, to be their best selves. And in fact, worship services trigger this same invitation: Worship recollects our highest values and names our aspirations—whether they're forgiveness, greening our homes, or fostering a deeper hunger in our lives for spiritual practice. We're summoned over and over to be the people we know that we can be, and to create the world we want to live in.

Worship should be carefully crafted and led by confident and skilled leaders—yet it needn't become a tyrannical quest for perfection.

Some people who consider joining this sermon-writing program offer conditions for their participation. "I'll be in the group if you promise that I don't have to actually get up in front of the congregation," they might say. This instinct to protect ourselves from the collective gaze shows how much courage is required to make ourselves visible and voice our private beliefs in front of those whose opinions we care about. Leading worship goes beyond courage, however—it requires vulnerability, which Brené Brown, a professor of social work, calls "the most accurate measure of courage."

Many of us assume that we're the only one who knows how much energy it takes to smile and move through life when we're dying on the inside. And yet, almost everyone has carried pain without daring to share it. We fear showing our soul's stripes; we fear appearing less than perfectly wise and absolutely poised. We fear making mistakes, whether it's losing our place in a written text, tripping on our way up to the pulpit, or saying something dumb.

If that sounds like you, I say: Channel your inner Julia Child. Take a page from the plucky chef who, on camera, would respond to dropping a chicken on the floor or a deflated soufflé with a shrug and a smile. Being vulnerable means being willing to take risks, and cozying up to the fact that we can't be sure everything will turn out okay. Leadership is the art of staying calm and centered even when our carefully laid out plan falls flat and we feel like running to the parking lot and driving away as quickly as possible. And finally, vulnerability is the capacity to shrug into the metaphorical camera, dust our hands off, and say (in words, if necessary), "Life is imperfect, and so am I. Let's move forward as we keep summoning grace and beauty."

Ready to Begin?

No matter how carefully this program has been planned, it's impossible to plan for every contingency—nor would I want you to. Your group will likely encounter moments of uncertainty or difficult decision-making as these sessions unfold. You'll find ways to shape this guide to your group's needs and style. Trust yourselves. Follow your covenant. If you find yourselves putting your energy into the things you fear, remind each other to serve your muse and your hopes instead.

May the hours in front of you hold laughter, tenderness, and gladness for you and your group.

Session 1

Writing a sermon is about finding your voice and your authority. What do you have to say that no one else can say?

Snapshot

In this first session, you will get accustomed to the flow of a gathering, clarify your expectations for the program, and get to know one another. Your discussion will center around what makes a sermon and what it means to have authority in the pulpit.

Welcome   5 minutes

Chalice Pages   15 minutes

Introductions and Overview   15 minutes

What brought you here?

Group Reading: What If?   5 minutes

I don't have anything to say.

Well, I do—but it might not be interesting to anyone.

I have secrets inside me, and struggles, and I don't know if I'm ready to share them.

> **What You'll Need**
>
> - your personal calendar
> - a pen or pencil
> - a journal, notebook, or other place to write

I want to hear what you have to say.

I want to speak of the deepest things together.

I want to hear what you dream about, what you hope for.

I want to know how you have come to arrive at this resting point along your journey.

What if I speak and you don't understand me?

I will listen, and listen again, until my hearing becomes understanding.

What if I can't find the words to share the world inside me?

I believe that wise words will emerge from you.

How can I trust you to hold my life's stories? You, who I may not even know?

By knowing that as I receive part of your story, I will give you one of mine.

How will this work? What will happen? What awaits us?

We can find out anything by beginning.

Let us begin to listen, and trust, and to know one another more deeply.

Lightning Interviews   10 minutes

First Pair: What's the best thing that happened to you in the past week?

Second Pair: Describe one of the most special objects (inanimate) in your home.

Third Pair: What's your favorite place to go when you want to be alone?

Fourth Pair: What does the word *spiritual* or *spirituality* mean to you?

Fifth Pair: Describe a question or issue you've been struggling with lately.

Expectations   10 minutes

Discussion: What Is a Sermon?   30 minutes

- What is a sermon?
- What makes a sermon different from a lecture or a presentation?

- Do you have feelings or associations with the word *sermon* that might get in the way of you crafting one?
- Think about sermons that you've heard. Which ones do you remember as being the most moving or meaningful? What makes a sermon memorable and meaningful to you?
- Complete this sentence: "At its most effective, a sermon makes me feel . . ."

Break   10 minutes

Discussion: Worship Authority in the Congregation   15 minutes

- In your congregation, who is responsible for worship services?
- In your congregation, who is accountable for worship services?
- How are these two lists different? What's the difference between responsibility and accountability?

Sample Worship Committee purpose statement:

1. To recognize the multiplicity of theologies and religious backgrounds in the congregation

2. To create a space and time that allows reverence

3. To create and support worship that engages the mind, touches the heart, and invites people to a new depth of spiritual development

4. To honor their roles as worship leaders in the congregation's shared ministry by speaking with one voice when interacting with the congregation

(This statement has guided the Worship Committee of Live Oak Unitarian Universalist Congregation in Goleta, California, since 2007.)

- How does this statement reflect responsibility?
- How does it reflect accountability?
- Does your congregation's Worship Committee or Sunday Service Committee have a mission or covenant?
- If so, how does it reflect the themes of responsibility and accountability?
- If not, what promises or intentions would you like those who plan your congregation's worship life to agree upon?

Group Reading: Authority in the UU Pulpit   25 minutes

One key aspect of Unitarian Universalism is our belief that ministry of the congregation does not belong exclusively to ordained clergy but to everyone.

Every person of faith has a ministry, and Unitarian Universalism, as a democratic faith, affirms what Martin Luther called the "priesthood of all believers." We are all lay ministers, whether or not we choose to be professional religious leaders.

Unitarian Universalism is a tradition of the free pulpit, which means that we invite the preacher—whether an ordained minister or a layperson—to give voice to the truth as he or she perceives it.

When we present a completed sermon to the congregation, we do not stand alone in the pulpit; we stand at the end of a long line of those who have proclaimed freedom, acceptance, and reason from the pulpit.

We have the example of great spiritual and moral leaders as well as words of poetry and scripture from across the ages to help us point toward the truths we are examining.

Our authority as speakers comes from more than five centuries of hard-won freedom, and all of the Unitarian and Universalist voices that have spoken their truth to the ears of the world.

Our authority to speak from the pulpit also comes from the gathered community: our congregation. By sharing in their authority, we speak on their behalf. We speak on behalf of all Unitarian Universalists.

It's a gift to receive the trust of our congregational leaders, who are accountable for the community's worship life.

When we speak our wisdom from a UU pulpit, we speak to many different people. We speak to the longtime members of our congregation who have created and sustained this community for us to enjoy.

We speak to newcomers who have only a foggy idea of what Unitarian Universalism is about and are curious to learn more.

We speak to the seekers, those who are hungry for meaning and purpose and are restless to find a spiritual home.

We speak to diehard Unitarian Universalists who are visiting from far-away congregations.

We speak to people with a diversity of beliefs and religious backgrounds.

We speak to our children and youth, who learn from us what it means to be Unitarian Universalists.

We speak to the people who are nursing broken hearts, those who are struggling with addiction or other inner demons, those who aren't certain that their lives matter.

May we each discover the wisdom that has shaped us, and the experience that has provided us with unique insight.

May we each discover that we have something to say that no one else can say.

May we each accept, and hold in trust, the authority we're given to speak our truth and preach our wisdom.

Discussion Questions

- What roles do you hold, or have you held, in the congregation?
- When have you felt empowered in those roles?
- Have you ever felt the sense of authority referred to in this reading? When?
- How have you understood the relationship between authority and the people who preach in Unitarian Universalist congregations?
- How is this different, if at all, from the religion or congregation of your childhood?
- What wisdom or experience has shaped you and provided you with unique insight?
- What do you have to say that no one else can say?

Review of Preparation for Session 2

- Read through Session 2.
- Write a reflection (200–300 words) to read out loud to the group. Write about an idea, belief, relationship, or experience that's uniquely yours. It doesn't have to be related to your presumed sermon topic. In fact, it might be better if it's not at all related so that you're free from the pressure of a far-away end product.
- Read "What Is Shared Ministry?" by Rev. Jan Carlsson-Bull (Reading A).
- Read "Writing to Be Spoken, Preaching to Be Heard" (Reading B).

Visit the Loose Ends List   5 minutes

Likes and Wishes   10 minutes
What did you appreciate about today's session? What would you like to see change?

Chalice Pages   15 minutes

What Is Shared Ministry?

Jan Carlsson-Bull

The notion of shared ministry comes from the early Christian concept of [what Martin Luther called] the "priesthood of all believers." In the early Christian church, there were no ministers, no priests. It was informal and egalitarian. Each believer was expected to draw on her or his distinctive gifts to build up the Christian community, not an easy task in that tumultuous time of the Roman Empire.

As Unitarians and Universalists, and, for the last half-century, as Unitarian Universalists, we have evolved as radical heretics—as a community committed to faith through choice as distinct from faith decreed through hierarchy. Congregational polity is a form of governance that formalizes this. Our congregations are in association with one another, but each chooses its own professional minister through a collaborative process with the minister and with the Unitarian Universalist Association of interdependent congregations.

It gets so muddy sometimes that I think a few Unitarian Universalists unwittingly long for a system that tells us which way is up, and more than a few refer to our Principles and Purposes with the solemnity of a creed. Yet we're ornery individualists struggling with all our might to be in or resist community.

Our religious community is covenantal, not creedal. It functions through a system of governance called congregational polity. Covenant and congregational polity blend into a soil fertile for shared ministry. Twentieth-century Unitarian theologian James Luther Adams extended that particular brand of shared ministry into the priesthood and prophethood of all believers. "The prophetic liberal church," Adams proclaimed, "is the church in which all members share the common responsibility to attempt to foresee the consequences of human behavior (both individual and institutional), with the intention of making history in place of merely being pushed around by it."

And just in case we didn't quite hear what he had to say the first time, he continued, "Only through the prophetism of all believers can we together foresee doom and mend our common ways."

In the late 1990s, a commission of our Association took on the task of pondering congregational polity. They drew feedback from congregations throughout our Association and talked and talked—after all it was a Unitarian Universalist committee—before committing to the written word. The fruit of this harvest was a rich narrative that moves into the sticky matter of religious leadership, which becomes more or less unsticky, depending on your perspective, through their agreed-upon observation that a common belief of Unitarian Universalists is "that ministry of the congregation does not belong exclusively to the ordained clergy, but to everyone."

We can either hear this as "Nobody's off the hook!" Or "We're all in it together!" Or both!

—adapted from the sermon "Shared Ministry: The Language of Listening"

Writing to Be Spoken, Preaching to Be Heard

Seasoned preachers intentionally approach their sermons as an oral/aural text rather than a written one. In fact, it's a growing trend in our UU ministry to prepare notes and reflections, but not write a full manuscript, before stepping into the pulpit. More and more clergy are eschewing written texts in order to make their sermons more immediate, more conversational, and more alive. In the words of Rev. Sonya Sukalski, "Humans have been listening to each other talk and telling stories for much much longer than they have been writing things down for each other."

It's still a wise practice for new preachers and sermon-givers to prepare their words well in advance and to read from a manuscript in the pulpit. Although the written page may tempt you to do otherwise, approach your sermon from the get-go as something to be spoken and heard, not read with the eyes. That requires some unique effort, if only to notice and set aside longstanding writing habits. Many of our UU congregants have careers that require them to write. Our UU congregations often include professors, teachers, scientists, and other professionals who write for specific audiences, often according to a specific style. Like radio announcers and playwrights, however, sermon-writers must consider how their language will sound to listeners' ears rather than "read" to people's eyes. (More and more congregations are posting only mp3 files of sermons, rather than text documents, to reflect ministers' understanding of this verbal art form.)

This can be challenging even for experienced clergy. Rev. Bill Gupton worked as a writer and editor for newspapers and magazines in his twenties. "When I eventually became a minister, the style of writing I used in crafting sermons was the same," he says, "and it made for pretty boring preaching. Then I made a drastic change—writing with repeats and refrains, adding conversational tone, emphasizing rhythm and cadence. I read aloud what I have written, using my 'preacher' voice, tone and cadence—and this results in some really good revisions with more flow and vocal power."

When asked for some other examples of how to mindfully orient their sermons for the voice and ear, seasoned UU clergy offered these tips:

1. More Like Hemingway, Less Like Faulkner

Keep sentences short. Vary the length so that there's variability from phrase to phrase, but don't let sentences run on and on and on. It's hard on the ear (and the brain) to follow sentences through multiple clauses.

2. Listen to How Words Sound

Sermon writers find themselves using poets' techniques, stringing words together to create what Robert Frost called the "sound of sense." As illustration, Frost's poem "Mowing" is filled with *ssss* sounds, mimicking the sound of his scythe in the grass. You may recall learning in those long-ago English classes about alliteration—the repetition of a consonant at the beginning of, or within, words in a phrase: "I <u>w</u>atched him as he <u>w</u>alked a<u>w</u>ay."

While these bits of flair shouldn't put undue stress on you and your writing process, they're effective flourishes on the final product. Nobody expects you to craft your sermon as though it were a graduate-level English project, but your listeners will respond, however unconsciously, to language whose sound reflects these nearly musical aspects.

As high-falutin' as this advice may sound, your sermon should sound like you. Speak in your language, with your mannerisms (those appropriate for a religious gathering, of course). Let people hear who you are and what your authentic voice sounds like.

3. Be Concrete

"Skip the conceptual," advises Rev. Martha Niebanck. "Use vivid sensory language." Most sermons employ Big Picture thinking, which requires abstraction ("Love is important"), and your listeners will need you to provide concrete illustrations and examples of your point. Try to include hooks in your sermon so that your listeners want to put themselves—their own lives and practices—into your frame of reference.

4. Build in Pauses

Every minister has learned that listeners appreciate pauses and brief silences. Too many words without enough pauses leave listeners frustrated that they couldn't follow you. Remember, you'll have spent many hours writing your sermon and will know it inside-out. Your listeners are hearing it for the first time. They'll need time to form their own images of your story and to process your language. Some words or phrases will need extra time to be understood. Pace your language. Your sermon, when read out loud, should not be fifteen or twenty minutes of solid speech.

Nor do you have to fill in every logical gap. Many listeners genuinely appreciate having space within a sermon so that they can apply their own experiences and questions to your words. Particularly in our Unitarian Universalist congregations, where we come from diverse traditions and life experiences, it's not the preacher's task to dot every existential *i* and cross every theological *t*. As Rev. Sean Dennison explains, "I leave 'fringes' on my sermons by not wrapping everything up perfectly—intentionally not getting too pedantic—and letting people have something they can fiddle with in their own minds. It may be a story that I don't spend too much time explaining or an image that I invoke, or a question that I allow to go unanswered. I think of this as 'leaving the wonderment in.'"

In other words, you're not expected to have The Answer, just an answer—yours—as your listeners find their way toward theirs.

5. Repetition Is Important

Many ministers structure their sermons spirally, not linearly: they circle back to their central point several times, perhaps adding nuances each time. If an image or phrase is foundational to your reflections, repeat it throughout the sermon. Repetition has more than one practical function. "Sometimes as a listener I drift off, chewing over an idea or image," admits Rev. Brian Kiely. "We need to leave people room to come back in easily by either making discrete points, or by repeating themes."

6. Details Draw Attention

When you're telling a story, details slow down your narrative pace and draw your listeners' focus. Use details to paint a picture for your listeners, but avoid extraneous details that confuse listeners about where you're headed.

Let's say that you want to tell a story about an encounter with a stranger at the airport. The point of your story is that when you first saw this stranger, you judged him to be a jerk, but then he surprised you with kindness and connection and you had to re-examine your own tendency to judge others. In telling such a story, you don't need to describe the turkey sandwich that you were eating, the magazine that you were reading at the gate, or what you were wearing (unless, say, your "Standing on the Side of Love" T-shirt is what sparked the encounter). Those details will slow down your listeners' attention as they wonder (consciously or unconsciously) whether the turkey sandwich is going to reappear later in the story, and how, and if not, why in the world you mentioned it. The more words you allot for description, the more you're tethering the congregation's focus (which requires energy from them). Don't spend all of your detail coins if you'll need to use them later for a more important point, the moment when the stranger went from Someone to Be Avoided to Someone Whose Kindness Opened Your Heart.

Here's an example of good use of details: "The slow wait at the airport cafe gave me enough time to look around at my fellow air travelers and see, among others, a guy wearing an NRA T-shirt. 'I hope he's not on my flight,' I thought to myself—a thought that disappeared when suddenly it was time to pay for my sandwich and go to my gate."

Or: "I had my head buried in a magazine, there at Gate 72, when a loud voice got my attention. It was a man I'd spotted earlier, and he was loudly complaining to his friend about poor people and how they're like 'parasites on this great nation.' His diatribe was so upsetting that I put away my magazine and took out my headphones, just to not have to keep listening to his judgmental rant."

7. Avoid Air Quotes

If you quote someone in your sermon, there are a number of ways to distinguish between your voice and theirs. Almost nobody likes to see a speaker use their hands to make so-called air quotes; not everyone can see them, either. Some people find it helpful, and others irritating, to hear a preacher say (for example), "As James Luther Adams reminds us, quote, 'Church is a place where you get to practice what it means to be human,' unquote."

There are more than a few ways to avoid the "quote sandwich." Some preachers lift the page of their manuscript when they read a quotation to signal that the words aren't their own. Others step to the side of the pulpit when they read, as if taking on the persona of someone else. Rev. Craig Schwalenberg alters his manuscript by putting quotes in different colors, reminding him to speak in a voice other than his own.

8. Make the Manuscript Work for You

No one will see your manuscript (at least not unless you allow them to, later). When it comes to ministers' sermon-writing practices, the most common counsel by far is to throw out the rules of written language—paragraphs, exact punctuation, one font—so that the text helps you preach as effectively as possible.

Grammatically, the spoken word is more flexible than written language. In a sermon, you can dangle participles, end sentences with prepositions, and begin sentences with *and* or *but*. If you find yourself writing your sermon with a stern but imaginary English teacher scowling over your shoulder, gently invite her to take her rules elsewhere so you can write with less inhibition.

Another way to make your manuscript work for you is to make liberal use of italics, bold face, and underlining. You can remove all or most of those changes if you're going to publish the piece, but while preaching, they can help you convey emphasis.

Another convention of written language eschewed by many preachers includes writing a sermon in paragraphs. "It just ain't right," says Rev. Matthew Johnson-Doyle.

Like many clergy, he devotes a single line of text to each phrase. A variation of this style is to type one line of text, indent the next, double-indent the third, and so on. As Rev. Rachel Anderson comments,

"This indenting allows me to prepare a manuscript
    that is more conducive to speaking.
It mimics transitions,
    pauses,
        and pace
                in a way that traditional paragraphs don't."

Breaking up sentences into separate lines means that you'll use more paper. Do it anyway. (The sermons in this book happen to have been printed in standard format because that's how their authors wrote and published them.)

9. Start Thinking about Your Delivery

Elsewhere in this book (Readings D and E) you'll find a list of suggestions to make your delivery as crisp and accessible as possible. This entails everything from the clothes you wear, to the kind of microphone you'll use, to what you should do if you have to sneeze. For the purposes of writing for the voice and the ear, begin to connect your words and stories to how they'll sound coming from your voice. Have you included names or words that you have trouble pronouncing? Can you comfortably speak for fifteen or twenty minutes while standing? (Try it, regularly.) Where in your body do you feel the energy of your sermon? Which sections of your sermon, if any, call for a louder, more fiery reading style, and which ones call for a gentler style?

Record yourself as you read your sermon drafts out loud, and listen to them. This suggestion is universally met with the protest, "But I hate the sound of my own voice!" Most of us do. Do it anyway. If you say "uuuuh" after every third sentence, drop your voice to an unintelligible level, or bore yourself with an unwavering pitch and tone, that's something you want to know (and work on) long before you get in the pulpit.

10. Honor Your Time Limit

Sooner or later, you might find yourself rebelling against the word restrictions suggested in this program. If you hit a streak of writing abundance, you may find it immensely challenging to whittle away content to leave a spare, 2,000-word sermon, making it tempting to deliver a longer one. You may even practice reading a 2,650-word sermon out loud and find that you can do it. While it's true that it's possible to read that quickly, it's very difficult for listeners to hear and to process more than 100 words per minute. If you've ever heard someone read a document at the speed of a runaway truck, you know how badly you want to pull an emergency auditory brake. Sermons should be heard, taken in, and thoughtfully digested. By honoring the word limit suggested here, you'll also be honoring your listeners' ability to take in your message.

Session 2

A sermon isn't about how much you know, or even what you know—it's about who you are. Who are you? What does your voice sound like?

Snapshot

This session begins with creating a covenant and includes a group conversation about the use of story and structure in sermons. You'll have your first opportunity to practice individual reading and responses. Overall, the session focuses on the emergence of your unique voice as your writing conveys your experiences and beliefs.

Chalice Pages   15 minutes

Haiku template
5 syllables_____
7 syllables _____
5 syllables _____

Reading of Haiku   5 minutes

Development of Covenant   20 minutes

- How do you want to be together?

What You'll Need

- a reflection (200–300 words)
- a pen or pencil
- a journal, notebook, or other place to write

- What do need, as support and encouragement?
- What will make you feel comfortable, safe, and valued?

Reading and Listening   80 minutes

- What images or words jumped out at you as juicy or compelling?
- What emotions did you hear in the reader's voice?
- Who is the person who emerges from the reflection?
- What do you most appreciate about the reflection?
- If the reflection included a story, which part of the story hooked you?
- What do you want to hear more about?

Break   15 minutes

Debriefing   5 minutes

What was the process of reading and providing feedback like for you?

Discussion: Who's Preaching?   15 minutes

When you read out loud and listened to each other's reflections before the break, how did you hear the person behind the writing? What did you learn about each other's beliefs, character, or experience?

Group Reading: Sermon Structure   15 minutes

Steps described in Richard C. Borden's book *Public Speaking—As Listeners Like It!*

Step One: Start a Fire!   In the first section of your sermon, grab your listeners' attention in the first sentence or paragraph. Tell them where you're going to take them as the sermon unfolds.

Step Two: Build a Bridge!   In the second section, make sure your listeners understand why you feel compelled to talk about this subject, and invite them to consider how it relates to them.

Step Three: For Instance!   In the body of your sermon, assert your beliefs but avoid putting the idea "in other words." Instead, illustrate your belief or point with a concrete story.

Step Four: Ask for Action!   The end of your sermon should have a point, answering your listeners' question "So what?" You might ask your listeners for some specific action: Join me. Reflect on this in your life. Watch for this theme in your daily actions. Commit to caring about this.

What other ways might you structure a twenty-minute sermon? If a story from your life is the center of a sermon, what might you layer around it?

Likes and Wishes   5 minutes

What did you appreciate about today's session? What would you like to see change?

Review of Preparation for Session 3

*   Read through Session 3.
*   Write a reflection (300–400 words) to read out loud to the group.
*   Read the first draft of the group's covenant and reflect on whether it conveys and promises what you need.
*   Read "Can't We Get Along? Loving Your (Political) Opponent" by Rev. Jessica Purple Rodela (Reading C).
*   Read "Do and Don't Tips for Crafting and Leading Worship," compiled by Rick Koyle (Reading D).
*   Read "Tips for Giving a Truly Terrible Sermon (50 Ways to Lose Your Listeners)" by Jane Rzepka and Ken Sawyer (Reading E).

Chalice Pages   15 minutes

Can't We Get Along? Loving Your (Political) Opponent

Jessica Purple Rodela

"It is not the symphony of voices in sweet concert I enjoy, but the cacophony of democracy, the brouhahas and the donny-brooks, the full-throated roar of a free people busy using their right to freedom of speech. Democracy requires rather a large tolerance for confusion and a secret relish for dissent. This is not a good country for those who are fond of unanimity and uniformity."

—Molly Ivins

"It would be difficult to name our reason for being if the privilege of non-conformity were denied or even threatened among us. By tradition and by practice we are dissenters. The cause of all dissent is our cause."

—John Haynes Holmes

> ## Start a Fire!
>
> Notice how Rodela begins her sermon: She paints a picture of a man who, by her own admission, is very different from her (and, frankly, from most Unitarian Universalists). Notice that she couches their differences in respectful and humorous terms.

Some eight years ago I had a neighbor, Bruce, who was a dyed-in-the-wool Marine Corps Master Gunnery Sergeant. By his own admission, he fit every stereotype of a bulldog, Rush Limbaugh-listening, war-mongering, church-loving, God-fearing, homophobic stentorian arch-conservative. According to Bruce, I am a tree-hugging, Birkenstock-wearing, pinko-commie, ACLU-loving liberal. It was natural, then, that when my son joined Bruce's Boy Scout troop . . . well, Bruce and I became fast friends.

Ours was a friendship that mystified a number of people, especially our spouses. Once a week the Boy Scouts would meet in my patio, while Bruce and I would sit at my kitchen table, drinking coffee, and discuss politics, religion, and family values . . . did I say "discuss"? Because we put the "cuss" in discuss. Our well-behaved spouses would retreat into the living room to discuss parenting and the neighbors. When our boys finished their meeting, they stood at the windows to eavesdrop, marveling at how such shouted argument could turn so fast into sure laughter.

But the only thing that came close to really angering me, frustrating me beyond the bounds of our ability to sit together, to "stay at the table" with one another in friendship, was Bruce's attitude toward compromise. He claimed that "if you compromise, then everyone loses. No one gets what they want."

It is this attitude that characterizes the great failure in political debate today—a failure embodied in the practice of partisanship. Partisanship is a committed bias to support one's special group interests above and beyond the wider good. Partisanship can be narrowly justified by loyalty, but it too often takes the form of "my party do or die, my people right or wrong." Such an uncompromising, unreasoned attitude is inherently unethical and theologically unsound. Unsound, because partisanship presumes dichotomy —and our complex lives transcend the simple dualism of right/wrong, either/or, us/them. And unethical, because Unitarian Universalist values require that we work for the common good—that we evaluate with reason, and judge with experience, every decision we make. As Unitarian Universalists, we cannot support the partisan idea that the ends justifies the means . . . for our liberal religion, the means matter. For us, revelation is not sealed, so truth is a process. Ours is a faith of questions, not answers. As such, we practice as spiritual goals resilience and a tolerance for ambiguity, and the ability to see simultaneously but differently.

Liberals and conservatives tend to see things simultaneously but differently—we see simultaneous ends, but with different means. At the core, I've found that my goals differ very little from those of my conservative neighbor's—ultimately, we aim to leave this world a better place than when we found it.

Where we differ is in radically different views about motivation and method. We differ on WHY we want to achieve these goals, and HOW we will do so, WHAT we are willing to sacrifice, and HOW we prioritize the steps, or means, to achieve the goal.

Prioritizing is a key issue in conflict management between cultures. According to something called Values Orientation Theory, there are only five universal values. Five big questions—about religion, law, finance, and community, that all human cultures are driven to explore. That's a lot of commonality. Yet, the vastly different ways we both prioritize and answer those five questions lead to interpersonal conflict, and can escalate into international war. The prioritizing of our values indicates what compromises—if any—we will make in order to establish peace.

The key to learning to love your opponents—political and otherwise—lies in distinguishing our differences. Perhaps that sounds counter-intuitive. The usual approach to learning to get along with one another is by oversimplifying our similarities and ignoring our differences, as we declare ourselves one big happy family, and we live tolerantly ever after . . . right?

Except it doesn't work that way. Instead, we easily see the destination we have in common, but when we disagree on *how* to get there, we feel mystified, even betrayed, at how "mistaken" our new friend can be, because they *seemed* so . . . intelligent, and if they just weren't so stubborn, or misinformed, or selfish, then they would see the light and we could get back to agreeing about how right I am. . . .

This cycle of events is repeated over and over again in heated family disagreements, and neighborhood circles, and our own church lobby. The failure to distinguish our divisions asks for inappropriate compromise. It tempts us to set aside differences instead of engaging them. We stand to learn far more from one another in investigating the

Build a Bridge!

Now that Rodela has our attention (perhaps she made you realize that there's a Bruce in your life, too), she uses this section to make it clear that personal conflicts play out on a larger scale. She also argues that it's not helpful to brush aside differences; only by acknowledging differences and sticking around to examine them—however uncomfortable that may be—can we get anywhere. Her language continues to model the tone of respect and curiosity that began the sermon.

boundaries of our differences, than had we tried to design each and every meeting, every initiative, or every worship service as "one size fits all." And such weak-kneed spirituality will lull our souls to sleep.

When we encounter our perceived opponents, and take the opportunity to engage with our differences, either in the world or within the walls of this church, our cherished assumptions are challenged. Divulging our differences requires that we better articulate our positions, and forces us to consider creative options we cannot see when we take a stand, only to face a mirror. Diversity enriches us by increasing our effectiveness in problem solving by widening our field of vision. In the martial art practice of tae kwon do, a master turns his body with the force of his opponent's attack, to gain leverage and advantage. Your opponent's agenda can be your own best friend.

History is full of ironies where the unexpected gift of an opponent serves what seems an opposite agenda. Who remembers that it was Richard Nixon who established the Environmental Protection Agency—reasoning that it was good for business!? And it was Democrat Bill Clinton, who became the conservative's friend when he signed Welfare Reform into effect—Clinton, who my husband deems, the "best Republican president we've ever had." Will anyone but my family remember my cousin Marcos, a well-respected Army officer, who registered as a conscientious objector while on active duty to protest our war in Iraq? Whether today, or tomorrow, we deem these actions a triumph or defeat, they serve as examples of why we must be willing and hopeful in working with those we oppose.

The promise and potential of working together lies in our willingness to remember to ask questions and stick around long enough to listen to the answers. That's all. It means when we talk, we do so with curiosity and compassion. It's about respect.

Educator Sharon Welch writes: "By respect we do not mean agreement, but taking someone so seriously that you ask why they think as they do." We have to stay at the table with one another, even when it is discouraging, or baffling, or inconvenient because diversity of opinions promotes dialogue. Without dialogue, there is no communication; without communication, there is no education; without education, there is no transformation.

A case in point: when the Boy Scouts of America began blatant discrimination against Unitarian Universalists in general, and against homosexuals in particular, my first reaction was to "take my boys and go home." But, without families like mine, the Boy Scouts of America would have no dialogue partner. They would be freed from our decent dissent. They would never change their policies, because they would never have them challenged. So, we were prepared—just like good scouting parents are told to be . . . when at a parent's meeting, that uncompromising Scout Leader, my friend Bruce, declared loudly that should the Scouts deem homosexuals as fit leaders, that would be the day he quits and "we'll just see what happens to this troop when men like me refuse to lead."

Without hesitation, my husband replied, "Well, then men like me will lead them," he said, with quiet firmness. "And this troop will continue, with or without you." And with that dozen words of dissent, the assumption and agenda in the room dissolved.

As disconcerting as conflict might feel, if we court only the like-minded, we stand no moderating influence, no witness to oppression. I suspect you agree with me so far. . . . That's all very well and good, you might say, but why must we do so in church?

I say to you that it is especially important to grapple with our differences in our churches, and especially appropriate for us as Unitarian Universalists. Because our politics reflects our values, and values create our religion, it is inescapable—even fitting—that these conflicts surface at church. That we employ separation of church and state is a necessary social evolution for a pluralistic community; but it does not negate the fact that religion is political. To separate religion from politics renders religion irrelevant and politics lethal. Every one of our seven Principles is a political statement, a paradigm of our values and beliefs. We do not turn to liberal religion in order to be told what to do but rather to be shown how to see. And we cannot—must not—learn where to look by only gazing at our own navels. If we create our church community as a monolith to agreement, we remove the checks and balances vital to our own spiritual growth and we rot in the stagnant pond of our assumptions; we stifle creativity when we are not called to the challenge. To practice choice, we have to be faced with something other than ourselves. As Sharon Welch writes: We need each other to be moral.

As Unitarian Universalists, our tradition enjoins us to a prophetic imperative, we affirm that theology IS practice, service is its prayer. Our religion IS social action. We stand for, work for, vote for—justice, equity and compassion. And the practical application of our faith is often expressed in our practice of politics.

Legendary minister and pacifist John Haynes Holmes climbed into his pulpit on the eve of World War I, knowing that he could lose his livelihood, knowing he was jeopardizing all he'd ever worked for. In the politics of the time, his views were considered treasonous. He delivered a fiery sermon, denouncing this and all war, as anti-Christian, and instead of a call for arms, he calls for alms; reconciliation; brotherhood.

The congregation responded with stunned silence. And Holmes left the pulpit for what he expected would be the last time. The Board president called an emergency meeting.

The church Board took two votes that evening. First, they unanimously condemned their minister's pacifism, declaring it to be dangerous, "wrong-headed," even treasonous. Second, they voted unanimously that, wrong-headed or not, John Haynes Holmes had an obligation to speak his mind. As Unitarians, they held dear our continuing tradition for right of conscience as expressed in our practice of freedom of the pulpit, a freedom that denies and defeats any possibility of succumbing to the tyranny of the majority; a freedom that recognizes a single dissenting voice as vital to the democratic process of a free and responsible search for truth and meaning.

Our oft-cited freedom in our faith, extends to our freedom of its expression. During annual commitment campaigns, you hear the challenge: "let your checkbook reflect your values." I extend that challenge today—to let the checkboxes on the ballot reflect your religious values as members of a liberal faith community. As Unitarian Universalists, our seven Principles require that we use the democratic process in ways that promote acceptance, spiritual growth, free and responsible search for truth and meaning, peace, liberty, and justice for all. We affirm the inherent worth and dignity of every person and thus uphold each one's right of conscience. But in doing so, we do not seek a collective conscience; nor does it imply that we must never take a public stand on controversial social issues. Our covenant guides us in how we make a decision as a community, rather than pointing to the decision itself. Our covenant to walk together guides our process, not the content.

Our devotion to diversity guarantees that our parent organization, the Unitarian Universalist Association, will make public sweeping statements that I and other clergy disagree with. It guarantees that from this pulpit, today, or tomorrow, you will hear messages from clergy you profoundly disagree with. Our promise of pluralism guarantees that this church institution will vote to take public stands that threaten or offend you . . . and for all that, I and you and they must, as Unitarian Universalists, stay at the table, because this is about conversation, not consensus. Conflict is inevitable.

It is part and parcel of the design of our free faith community, bound together, not by creed, but by covenant. And by courting that difference, by hosting it here, in our beloved community, we are informed and transformed by diversity. There is fear, I know, a legitimate fear, that if Horizon UU church takes public stands on social issues, it will cost us—in membership and in pledge money. But I guarantee—and our history guarantees—that if you think it costly to take a stand . . . the costs of not taking one are far higher. We can choose to turn from or learn from adversity . . . but we can only do that if we consent to conflict. And in today's fearful national climate, it is more important than ever that we be willing to stand up for our right to a decent dissent.

In his time, the Reverend John Haynes Holmes was vilified for his pacifism. Today we acclaim Holmes as a prophet and hero. He is. But I also acclaim that brave church Board who had the moral courage to vote their religious values above their partisan views and despite looming congregational conflict. In so doing, they created a compromise through covenant, declaring that by staying in relationship with our (political) opponents, we get along much better. In such a compromise, all of us win.

This is our legacy. This is Unitarian Universalism.

Ask for Action!

In Rodela's final section, she makes the case that courting difference and daring to disagree has moral and spiritual implications. She invites her congregation to view itself not as an isolated church but rather as connected to a longstanding tradition of bold justice-making and truth-telling.

Do and Don't Tips for Crafting and Leading Worship

The following list is adapted from The Shared Ministry Sourcebook, *edited by Barbara Child. It was assembled by Rick Koyle from many sources, including Mark Belletini, Janne Eller-Isaacs, Rob Eller-Isaacs, Judith Hunt, Heather Macleod, Rebecca Parker, Maud Steyaert, the class in worship at Starr King School for the Ministry in Spring 1993, and worship associates at the First Unitarian Church of Oakland.*

DON'T begin: "As I was pondering what to say . . ." Just say it. Exception: where the pondering is an integral part of your story.

DON'T run to the dictionary for a definition. It has become a cliché. Exception: Etymologies are fine. But "Webster's tells us . . ." is a bore.

DON'T apologize. You're a child of God or the universe. There is nothing to apologize for.

DO take care of your congregation. They are really yours. They have placed themselves in your care for an hour. Some are hurting. Some are angry. Some need sympathy, others to be challenged, others just to laugh or cry. Try to make worship a safe place for them all.

DO over-rehearse. DON'T try to wing it until you've been doing this every week for, say, ten years. Maybe not even then.

DON'T draw attention to yourself. The message counts, not the messenger.

DO, however, share something of yourself. If you can, try to say something that costs you something to say.

DO take a risk, provided you can do so worshipfully. Have faith. If you don't have faith during worship, why are you up there?

DO pray or meditate beforehand. You need all the help you can get.

DO remember what you are there for and what you are doing in the pulpit.

DON'T assume everyone knows what you're talking about. Invite the whole congregation under the tent.

DON'T put anybody down, including yourself. The God, if there is a God, who loves you might be offended.

DO respond to whatever unusual happens during your sermon. If a person in a wheelchair enters through the side entrance in mid-sermon, pay no attention. If the goat with that person wanders up to the altar and starts eating the flowers, you have to pay attention. Appropriately acknowledge the intrusion, and move on. (Confronted with a goat, DON'T try to improvise a ritual sacrifice. It might be okay to make a joke about it. Just don't ignore it. Worship is not about pretending the world is other than the way it is. Good worship faces facts.)

DO relate all past and future, all anecdotes and tales and schemes and visions, to the present—right here, right now. Let worship make a difference.

DON'T overexplain. Worship is creation, not commentary, action rather than criticism.

DON'T yield to the temptation to explain why you are doing it this way rather than some other way. No one cares, nor should they. The world doesn't care about the birth pains; all it wants to see is the baby.

DO accept that, in most worship services, many small things are bound to go wrong, and yet at the same time, mysteriously, nothing whatsoever will go wrong. Whatever you do with a worshipful attitude will work out fine.

DO take pains. Attention to details equals love.

Tips for Giving a Truly Terrible Sermon (50 Ways to Lose Your Listeners)

Jane Rzepka and Ken Sawyer

For many years, Revs. Jane Rzepka and Ken Sawyer led a popular preaching seminar for UU ministers. Among the resources they gave their students was a list of reverse tips for giving a truly terrible sermon, an exhaustive collection of the worst preaching practices found in Unitarian Universalism today.

1. Make it longer than they expect.

2. Preach mostly about yourself.

3. Mumble.

4. Assume that you are more spiritually evolved than they are. Try to bring them along.

5. Ignore the service around the sermon.

6. Choose a topic that only you care about.

7. Crude language helps.

8. Exclude some parishioners with your theology.

9. Have no religious point.

10. Tell a personal story about someone without permission.

11. Count on inspiration to show up when you want it to.

12. Don't acknowledge Unitarian Universalism.

13. Preach without including any actual ideas.

14. Toss in lots and lots of images, stories, and quotes.

15. Assume that good grammar is for fuddy-duddies.

16. Apologize.

17. Depend on one book as a basis for your sermon; quote from it a lot.

18. Assume that the sermon will carry itself without need of stories or humor.

19. Show off your impressive vocabulary.

20. Ignore local context and world events; preach generic sermons.

21. Presume that everyone there shares the same assumptions, experience, background, politics, and level of privilege.

22. Brag.

23. No one cares if you can't really sing; break into song in the midst of your sermon.

24. Use a string of clichés.

25. Don't look at anyone.

26. Gratuitous manipulation of their feelings is always appreciated.

27. Whine.

28. Keep them abreast of your children and pets with amusing tales.

29. Wait until the last minute to print your sermon.

30. Point weak, pound pulpit.

31. Use corny props.

32. Take time to tell how brief you'll be.

33. Talk about your favorite subject regularly.

34. Use long quotes and be unclear about when they begin and end.

35. Spring back, fall forward.

36. Assume that theological language and ritual from your own past is appreciated by everyone.

37. Feel confident that extemporaneous preaching is best.

38. Pompousness is good.

39. Pick an idea that's too big or too small to be a sermon's subject.

40. Presumptuously and erroneously speak of "we" and "us."

41. Let special interest groups control your preaching calendar.

42. Scold them.

43. Inexplicably, smile all the time.

44. Fail to provide even a shred of good news.

45. Let your accessories do the talking.

46. Sway.

47. Don't test the mike.

48. Stick to your text, no matter what.

49. Make the star of the crucial story, you.

50. Focus on delivering a great sermon rather than speaking to the hearts and minds of your [fellow] parishioners.

Note: Observant readers may find surface dissonance between Tips 2 and 49 and this program's emphasis on turning a story from your life into a nuanced spiritual reflection. It's one thing to fall into a pattern of self-aggrandizing "all about me" moments—the verbal equivalent of doing a cannonball into the worship vessel. It's quite another thing to choose a story from your own struggles and place it before the congregation, with care and mindfulness, as a lens for their own reflection. In worship, the preacher is a channel or conduit for their own (or another's) wisdom, not the star of a one-person monologue.

Session 3

What freedom and creativity remain within limitations?
What images or metaphors are appearing in your sermon?

Snapshot

In this session, you'll explore the nuts and bolts of worship, including a discussion of whether there are rules for preaching and, if so, why they might be helpful. You'll also reflect on three important guidelines for the caring exercise of authority in a sermon. Between this session and Session 4, you'll also consider how an image and/or metaphor can anchor your sermon, engaging senses beneath the intellect to bring your message home.

What You'll Need

- a reflection (400–600 words)
- a pen or pencil
- a journal, notebook, or other place to write

Chalice Pages   15 minutes

Creating Your Own Prayer/Meditation
(exercise by Rev. Lisa Ward)

Oh _____, _____, _____, _____
                (three descriptors)   (subject)

I know you _____.

Sometimes I fear _____.

(Ask "it" a question) _____?

Thank you for _____.

(Repeat 1st line:) Oh _____, _____, _____, _____.

Reading of Prayers/Meditations   10 minutes

Review of Covenant   10 minutes

Discussion of Reading C   10 minutes

Setting aside whether you liked Rodela's sermon (Reading C) or not, did the four sections make sense to you? Did they sound natural? Did you hear (or see) her sermon pivot according to the four stages of the Borden method?

What other ways might you fit together a personal story and big picture reflection in your sermon?

How do you think sermon structure relates to the sound of someone's written voice? Where does the person—you, as the sermon-writer—appear and then move into the background so that the idea can take center stage?

Reading and Listening   70 minutes

- Where does the writer appear? Where does the writer move into the background so that the ideas can take center stage?
- Did any images or metaphors appear in the writer's story?
- Where did the reader risk being vulnerable?
- What do you want to hear more about?

Break   10 minutes

Group Reading: Three Good Guidelines   15 minutes

Our faith tradition extends beyond traditional religious boundaries. We don't limit ourselves to a creed, for example, nor do we limit our scripture to a single book. Since our faith is expansive, some Unitarian Universalists are uncomfortable with applying limits or rules to our worship experience. However, this reading highlights three guidelines that are fundamental to claiming your authority and using it with thoughtful responsibility.

It should go without saying that responsible, respectful worship leaders never mock or disparage another religion—a practice that, embarrassingly, has been all too common in our past. More than one UU has brought friends of another faith to experience worship at their church, only to hear the preacher or another worship leader speak pejoratively about that very same faith. It's one thing to thoughtfully counter another religion's theology or to reflect on past injuries inflicted by a faith community, but snide comments fail to embody the acceptance—let alone tolerance—that we claim to practice. Respect is called for, if only on principle (or Principle!), but it's also true that we never know who's sitting in the pews. Let your sacred self reign.

Every Sunday, Someone's Heart Is Breaking

People come to church for many reasons; often they come with an unresolved grief or a fresh sorrow. Many newcomers report that they'd intended to attend a Unitarian Universalist service for a while but were finally spurred to visit because of some pain or crisis in their lives. Since people hunger for a sense of community when their lives are painful, offering hope is a central purpose of worship. Roman Catholic theologian Paul Wadell says,

> When he was writing about the virtue of hope, St. Thomas Aquinas said we are much more inclined to be hopeful when we have friends to rely on. . . . Hope has to be seen to be believed. It has to be made visible. It has to be something we can feel and touch. . . . We are called to be persons who embody hope for one another. . . . We have to be each other's partners in hope.

Other elements in a worship service are designed to minister to the breaking hearts in the room, of course, but as you write your sermon, remember that your words should embody hope.

Don't Tell Someone Else's Story

Stories give life to sermons. Our lives are filled with funny, outrageous, chilling, evocative, and *true* stories that provide rich material for sermons. A good story can move hearts, draw tears, and powerfully illustrate a concept.

Often, our stories involve other people. It's a great idea to build a sermon around a story taken from your life *if* the people involved are comfortable being named. Asking people for their permission before we tell stories about them communicates respect for those relationships. No one should ever be surprised by hearing a story about themselves—or reading it—in a sermon, even if you think the story is inoffensive or even flattering. This is especially true now that many congregations post sermon texts and podcasts on their websites. This rule applies to family members, including children.

Consider the following four pairs of statements. In each pair, one statement doesn't need permission while the other shouldn't be shared without the consent of the person involved.

1. No permission problem: "Being part of this congregation has taught me how to stay in relationship during times of conflict."

STOP! Permission required: "Last year, Ginger and I had a huge fight when she supported the building proposal and I was opposed to it. It took us months to put the conflict behind us and repair our friendship."

2. No permission problem: "I feel strongly about marriage equality because I have family members who are gay. It hurts me that they can't enjoy the gifts and privilege of legal marriage."

STOP! Permission required: "My aunt, Tracy Gannett, is a lesbian and has been in a civil union with her partner, Joan McDonnell, for eight years."

3. No permission problem: "I know what it feels like to be betrayed and to believe that forgiveness will never be possible."

STOP! Permission required: "I had to learn about forgiveness when my wife cheated on me three times in seven years."

4. No permission problem: "Parenting my children has been a difficult but richly rewarding experience."

STOP! Permission required: "My teenage son, Andrew, is so hard to live with that we go to family therapy twice a week."

If you can't get someone's permission—if, for example, they're deceased or they've disappeared from your life and you don't know how to reach them—use your best judgment about whether you should refer to that person with a pseudonym.

No Meta-Talk

The prefix *meta* (Greek for "self") indicates conversation "about the about." In the context of this program, meta-talk applies to language in a sermon that refers to your feelings about your sermon, what the first drafts of your sermon were like, the time or word constraints of your sermon, your feelings about those time or word constraints, your apologies for a sermon's quality . . . . Get the picture?

A sermon isn't about how much you know or even what you know—it's about who you are: You are a channel, or vessel, for your message. Meta-talk shifts the focus away from you as the vessel to you as a person. It creates holes in your vessel, through which your authority leaks away. As Rev. Victoria Weinstein puts it, "Extraneous chatter . . . disturbs the flow, interrupts the worship experience, and communicates anxiety and lack of preparedness, experience and depth."

Imagine suffering from an acute health need and learning that you need a procedure in order to heal. Now imagine your doctor saying, "I'm really nervous because I've never done this procedure before. It took me a long time to learn how. I'm worried that I might make a mistake. Please bear with me." Would you feel confident in your doctor? Would he or she seem professional? Would you look forward to that medical procedure? Not likely.

Here are some examples of meta-talk, their subtext, and alternatives:

1. Meta-talk: "I'm really nervous."

The Subtext: "I don't have much confidence in my authority to speak, so you shouldn't either."

Instead, Try This: Take a breath. Drop your shoulders. Find a smiling, friendly face in the crowd.

2. Meta-talk: "I hate speaking in public."

The Subtext: "I don't want to be here. Why should you want to be here either?"

Instead, Try This: Claim your ground. Center yourself and remember that you have a right to speak.

3. Meta-talk: "It was really hard to write this sermon. I've spent a lot of time on it."

The Subtext: "I need you, the congregation, to take responsibility for my anxiety."

Instead, Try This: Trust your voice and your process. Preach your message.

4. Meta-talk: "I spent all summer writing my sermon, but last week, I decided to tear it up and start all over from scratch."

The Subtext: "I'm sorry if you don't like this sermon. Please ask me about my first sermon."

Instead, Try This: Let your first sermon go. Be present and committed to this one.

5. Meta-talk: "It was hard to choose which story to tell you today. There are so many stories that could illustrate my point."

The Subtext: "I'm sorry that I didn't find a clearly illustrative story. Please ask me about the other stories."

Instead, Try This: "Here's a story that illustrates this dilemma . . ."

6. Meta-talk: "I had to cut a lot out of my sermon to stay within my time limit. It was harder than I thought—I have so much to say."

The Subtext: ". . . and I am using up my valuable words to describe my process instead of delivering my sermon."

Instead, Try This: Use your words carefully, so they count as much as possible.

7. Meta-talk: "Writing this sermon was one of the hardest things I've ever done. I'd never spent so much time thinking about forgiveness."

The Subtext: Start the violins!

Instead, Try This: "When I began to reflect deeply on the topic of forgiveness, many of my relationships were transformed."

Discussion of Group Reading   20 minutes

- What are the intentions behind these rules and guidelines?
- What kind of expectations are being named or hinted at?
- Which guidelines leapt out at you, either because they're obvious or because you've never considered them before?
- Would you add any other rules to the list?

Likes and Wishes   5 minutes

What did you appreciate about today's session? What would you like to see change?

Review of Preparation for Session 4

- Read through Session 4.
- Write a reflection (600–800 words) to read out loud to the group. You can elaborate on a reflection you've already read, or shift to a different subject. Choose an experience, belief, or subject that you're especially drawn to. If your previous reflections haven't yet been very personal—telling your story, describing your beliefs, sharing your experience—take the risk of writing in this way.
- Read "Treasured Dishes, Fragile Cups," by Rev. Patrick T. O'Neill (Reading F). As you read, consider how O'Neill uses the image of china as a lens for viewing our emotional lives.
- Read "Images and Metaphors" (Reading G).
- Read "Energy in the Transitions" (Reading H).

Chalice Pages   15 minutes

Treasured Dishes, Fragile Cups

Patrick T. O'Neill

Our Jeopardy

It is good to use
best china
treasured dishes
the most genuine goblets
or the oldest lace tablecloth
there is a risk of course
every time we use anything
or anyone shares an inmost
mood or moment
or a fragile cup of revelation
but not to touch
not to handle
not to employ the available
artifacts of being
a human being

that is the quiet crash
the deadly catastrophe
where nothing
is enjoyed or broken
or spoken or spilled
or stained or mended
where nothing is ever
lived
loved
pored over
laughed over
wept over
lost
or found.

—Thomas John Carlisle

Reading Carlisle's poem, I was thrown back to a day, gosh, almost thirty years ago now, when I was serving my first little congregation out in the Yakima Valley of Washington State. On this particular day, I got a call from a local farm family telling me their mother had died, and asking if I would come do a burial service for their mother. They were not church people themselves, but, you know how this works, their next door neighbor had once been a Unitarian Universalist, and he recommended they call me.

She was an elderly woman, many years a widow, and she and her husband were among the early farming families of the area, and in fact they had become quite wealthy over the years. The land that she and her husband had bought so cheaply in the 1920s, and on which they had barely survived through the Great Depression years, turned into something of a goldmine in the 1940s when they irrigated it and discovered that apple trees fared exceptionally well in that volcanic soil.

Within twenty years or so after World War II, Washington State apples were world-renowned, and the Yakima and Wenatchee Valleys were at the center of a worldwide agribusiness. And so it was that this woman and her husband, who always lived quite modestly, managed to leave their children a sizable fortune.

When I arrived at the house that evening to meet with the family and plan the funeral service, the woman's grown daughter was sitting in the living room with several cartons and crates opened in front of her, and she was weeping softly.

"I just found these in the closet," she said, "two full sets of Wedgwood china from England that my mother apparently ordered from a catalog thirty years ago, and then promptly stored away in the back closet. They have never been used, not even once. In fact, they have never even been taken out of the boxes they came in, even to be looked at. I find that so sad," she said. "My mother was so afraid that she might chip or break even a single plate that she never once dared to take them out of the carton. That's how she was. That's so typical of our Mom."

Because I never knew the old woman personally, I've always wondered about those beautiful unused dishes. The daughter saw them as symbolic of her mother's over-cautious approach to life, and perhaps she was right. But I've always wondered if that was the real story. Adult children always think they know their parents so well, but sometimes they don't know their parents nearly as well as they suppose.

Was that old woman really so fearful of damaging these beautiful things that she would not even put them out where she could enjoy looking at them? That really would be sad if it were true.

Or did the dishes perhaps represent something else for that old woman? For this farmwoman who had survived years when she and her family had endured near-destitute poverty, were these exquisite dishes perchance some secret insurance against the return of hard times? Her personal barter, perhaps, against the years of drought and failed crops that she had known years before and wanted never to revisit?

Or could it be that these elegant place settings were a forgotten hope chest, perhaps ironically meant for the very daughter who now judged her and wept at her mother's choice of caution over enjoyment in life?

Or were they something else, these dishes? The one impulsive gesture of extravagance, perhaps, stored away in a closet, by a woman whose whole life was otherwise a model of moderation and restraint?

We'll never know, of course. And neither will her daughter ever know for sure. But whatever story really accounts for the beautiful unused dishes, don't you just wish that in all those years, the woman had found it within herself, at least once, to splurge a little—oh, some afternoon when no one else was around, maybe, or better yet, in the shared company of an old friend, or with her daughter—don't you wish she had just served herself at least one incredibly elegant cup of tea, with one wonderful little dessert perhaps, on that exquisite chinaware?

Wouldn't you hope she would have dared it one day, risked it all, thrown caution to the wind, and just for the sheer living of it, allowed herself to make bold use of the beauty and craft of those treasured dishes, those fragile cups?

Oh, I say it not in judgment, but as a wish for her, and for us all. I say it for all those moments in our lives when we, too, are afraid of using the best that is in us, the good stuff that we keep locked away inside us like chinaware in a closet.

I say it for all those moments in all our lives, when—for fear of breakage, for fear of failure, for fear of rejection, or being hurt, or being laughed at—we, too, choose safety over adventure. We choose retreat into the dead habits of status quo, rather than choosing the challenge of growth and new learning for ourselves.

The times when we choose the safety of silence over the risk of expressing our love and our need of others. The times when we choose isolation over relationship, because we're afraid to let someone else know who we are and how it really is with us.

We've learned over time, many of us, to keep our hearts under wraps, carefully packed away where no one can even see them, let alone misuse them or break them. Like this farmwoman who lived through the Great Depression, and who forever after lived her life out of a "scarcity mentality," afraid to enjoy or employ the most beautiful possessions she had for fear that she might possibly lose them or break them, too many of us, too many of us, live our lives out of a similar scarcity mode.

Living in scarcity mode, you realize, has nothing to do with how much money or how many assets you have, how rich you are or how poor you might be materially. Living in scarcity mode means living constantly in negative energy. It means living a miserly existence, in constant awareness of all the things we lack, all the things we think we don't have enough of, all the things we want more of. It means living fearfully and anxiously, in fear of losing what we have, in fear of giving too much of ourselves away and someday perhaps not having enough for ourselves.

It's difficult for scarcity people to give their time or their money or their energy or their loyalty to anyone else, even to people they say they love, even to causes they claim to believe in. I always remember one of the harshest indictments I ever heard anyone issue was from a woman who described her husband as an "emotional miser," a man completely unable to share a tender moment or give a loving compliment to anyone around him.

It's the opposite, of course, with people who live in abundance mode. People who live in abundance mode live in positive energy. They are aware of all that they have, all the ways in which their lives are blessed. They have no fear of giving themselves to others or to good works and great causes, because they know the one great secret of spiritual living, the one that Francis of Assisi is said to have spoken of in the famous prayer which declares that it is in giving that we receive.

Abundance people have their good china unpacked and on display, because they learned long ago that that's what good china is for!

How is it with you these days? Are you living your life from a scarcity mode or an abundance mode? If your family were asked that question about you today, how would they respond? How would your children describe you? If your friends and fellow workers and neighbors were asked to describe you in these terms, what would they say about you? Would they call you a scarcity person or an abundance person?

Our Unitarian Universalist faith isn't about teaching people how to live more miserly spiritual lives. Our faith is about helping people to live more abundant lives, more generous lives, more giving lives. Our church isn't about teaching people to live more timidly, more fearfully, more guardedly in the world. Church should call each of us to live and to love more bravely in this wounded world, more courageously, more daringly.

That is, I think, what most of us hope for when we identify as Unitarian Universalists. We hope that somehow, in some significant way, our lives will be enriched. Be touched. Maybe even be transformed.

We come to Unitarian Universalism hoping it will bring greater abundance to our lives: spiritual, emotional, intellectual, aesthetic, communal abundance. Our church should call us to live our lives from that sense of abundance, with a greater appreciation and a greater awareness and use of all the best that is in us—the good stuff inside each of us, the good china, if you will, that we tend to keep locked away much of the time—our best talents, our deepest loves, our highest ideals and hopes and dreams.

When a church community is truly living in such an abundance mode, there is no limit to what it can do and become as a community of transformation. And if a church community is not willing to do that, then nothing else much matters. A church living in scarcity mode will always just be running in place anyway.

So, here, then, is a little spiritual exercise for you to try this week. (And you thought being a Unitarian Universalist meant never having to do spiritual exercises. . . .) But I must warn you: This one takes courage, and it is not without risk!

Some afternoon this week, or perhaps some early morning, when there is no one else around, go ahead and take down the nicest cup in the house, and have yourself a cup of tea! Have it in memory of a farmwoman from Yakima, Washington, whom you never met. And while you're doing that, give thanks for the many blessings and tender mercies that mark your life.

Images and Metaphors

"In the beginning was the Word . . . ." So begins the Gospel According to John, as the author creates an alternate name for Jesus. The phrase points backward to the first chapter of Genesis, in which God summons creation by nothing more than speaking. Both authors suggest that the "Word" had an existence even before the world was made, when there was nothing.

Today, few Unitarian Universalists view Biblical scripture as central to their spiritual path—and yet the Christian worship tradition is a main source that informs the way we UUs worship today: The sermon usually serves as the hearty "entrée" of worship, accompanied by a few small side dishes.

In a sermon he delivered in 2011, Rev. Bruce Marshall points out the degree to which our UU worship reflects the centuries-old worship practices of the New England Puritans:

> For the New England Puritans, the purpose of their worship was to interpret— to seek to understand—the word of God as revealed in the Scriptures. The point in the service where that occurred was the sermon. For the New England Puritans, the sermon was the main event of worship. It was through the sermon that they sought insight into the ways of God and how God interacts with the world. . . . Whenever today's UU congregations are surveyed as to what's most important to them in worship, just about all will give top priority to the sermon. Lots of other things happen in worship that people value, but it's the sermon that makes it or breaks it. . . . Like the Puritans of New England, we are people of the Word.

As Unitarian Universalists, our worship services (including sermons) tend to be word-heavy. Many of us expect meaty, thought-provoking services that will give us material to chew on, mentally, for the week ahead. Yet when we over-emphasize the Word, we risk falling short of worship's potential to reach into people's hearts and bodies, not just their minds. (Who reading this hasn't heard—or, like me, written—at least one sermon so densely worded that it made us want to weep, and not in a good way?)

First, even practiced sermon-writers can fall into the trap of writing a sermon as though it is meant to be read rather than heard out loud (see "Writing to Be Spoken, Preaching to Be Heard," Reading B).

Second, many sermons revolve around themes. Whether the theme applies to the morning on which the sermon is delivered or to an entire month of worship, these themes are often abstract, broad enough to encompass different interpretations (think justice and motherhood). However, weaving an abstract or vague theme through a sermon can also deprive listeners of the ability to hook their attention on a precise, clear message.

Finally, word-heavy, linguistically embellished sermons—even when they're elevated by poetic language—fail to acknowledge the diversity of learning styles in our congregations. Unitarian Universalists frequently—and admirably—voice their hope for greater diversity in our congregations. It goes without saying that we should never stop longing for racial and cultural diversity. Among the many ways to be "diverse," there's already an invisible and often forgotten diversity present in our congregations every Sunday: the many different ways that people take in and process information to make sense of the sermon and of the world.

In her book *Learning Styles: Reaching Everyone God Gave You*, Marlene LeFever cites research conducted among sixth graders. Out of every ten learners, scientists have found, there are:

- 2 primarily auditory learners, who learn and make meaning by listening
- 4 primarily visual learners, who learn and make meaning by watching
- 4 primarily tactile kinesthetic learners, who learn and make meaning by moving their bodies.

Adult Unitarian Universalists may not reflect the same ratios as the sixth graders in this study. Nevertheless, not everyone takes in and processes information in exactly the same way. Why would we expect a word-rich sermon to feed everyone in the congregation—particularly when it's framed in broadly abstract terms?

In her groundbreaking approach to sensory-rich worship, United Methodist worship leader Marcia McFee encourages worship leaders to approach the central image or lesson in three ways: verbally, visually, and viscerally (feel it, participate in it). We know how to do verbal. The visceral approach can be complicated and nuanced. Weaving the visual into a sermon and the rest of the worship service, however, is a simple but powerful way to layer the senses and engage the worshipping community more effectively.

As you shape your sermon and the worship elements that will complement it, consider stepping away from abstract themes; instead, funnel the worship experience through a visual lens. What image or metaphor might subtly convey (or replace) its central theme? How might you convey the deeper meaning through the language of an image?

For example, one of the most beloved poems in the American canon is Robert Frost's "The Road Not Taken," with its famous image of a hesitating narrator standing at a crossroads who admits that no matter which road he takes, he'll wonder about the unexplored route long after it's behind him.

The Road Not Taken
Robert Frost

Two roads diverged in a yellow wood,
And sorry I could not travel both
And be one traveler, long I stood
And looked down one as far as I could
To where it bent in the undergrowth;

Then took the other, as just as fair,
And having perhaps the better claim,
Because it was grassy and wanted wear;
Though as for that, the passing there
Had worn them really about the same,

And both that morning equally lay
In leaves no step had trodden black.
Oh, I kept the first for another day!
Yet knowing how way leads on to way,
I doubted if I should ever come back.

I shall be telling this with a sigh
Somewhere ages and ages hence:
Two roads diverged in a wood, and I—
I took the one less traveled by,
And that has made all the difference.

If you were to ask ten Unitarian Universalists to list the meanings behind a generic topic like choices or fate, their answers would vary widely—but if those same ten people were invited to think of an unforgettable place where "two roads diverged" in their lives, a doorway to common experience would open. Even as we encounter the appeal of freedom offered by choices, we're burdened with the knowledge that in order to keep moving, we must cut off possibility, with its allure of the Unknown. To look back and wonder about what might have been—whether it's with a sigh, sadness, or satisfaction—is a universal part of the human journey.

The use of a powerful image or metaphor doesn't necessarily apply to the sermon alone; it can be even more important to use in the worship service as a whole. The back of *Singing the Living Tradition*, for example, distributes hundreds of our hymns into dozens of themes and categories. Few of those categories are as useful as we imagine them to be.

Consider a sermon about our faith-full anti-oppression work. Most worship leaders would pack a sermon with verbal material, and employ hymns that fall under the hymnal's Justice theme. There's nothing wrong with this approach per se, but it risks leaving the listener swimming in a slurry of words, words, words. The hook of a metaphor can provide meaning and anchor the worship service in people's memory. There's a reason that most of us refer to Martin Luther King Jr.'s most famous speech as "The Mountaintop," its metaphor.

To apply "The Crossroads" or "The Mountaintop" approach to an anti-oppression service, begin by combing through the sermon or an indispensable hymn for images. What speaks to you? What resonates inside your gut, your spirit, as capturing your message? Is it a cage? (If so, what kind? An ornate, gilded birdcage or the sturdy bars of a zoo?) Is it a billowing, shimmering silk canopy, under which all are welcome? Is it a banquet table filled with nourishing food at which all are welcome? Whatever you decide, there's a hymn for that!

Don't limit this brainstorming process to the private confines of your own imagination. Ask for help. Doodle. Talk out loud. Once you settle on a satisfying image or metaphor, search our hymnals for your image—either the word or its variations. If you use the image of a Welcome Table, for instance, you can find more hymns to use by searching for words like *banquet, feast, feed,* or *hunger.* Rely on people in your congregation who know the hymnal inside-out, or spend some time reading through hymns, scanning all verses for the metaphors (sometimes the third or fourth verse contains a dazzling, apt image). You might even explore the cyber-world, available at your fingertips, to discover music and worship resources from other faith traditions.

Once you've settled on an image or metaphor with a strong visual component, brainstorm about how it can be made visceral (how to help people feel it, participate in it, taste it, smell it). Don't be afraid to try something that's never been done before. If you take risks reverently and responsibly, chances are you'll reach your congregation in new ways.

Some examples:

THEME	IMAGE/METAPHOR	SAMPLE WORSHIP ELEMENT	ONE WAY TO MAKE IT VISCERAL
immigration justice	water in the desert; thirsting for justice	"De Noche," *Singing the Journey* #1034	Stack plastic water jugs on the chancel as reminders of how border-crossers stay alive in the desert.
caring for the human family (or Guest at Your Table)	bread as sustenance; for a global emphasis, breads of the world	Guest at Your Table materials from the Unitarian Universalist Service Committee	Program a bread machine or toaster oven to bake so that the smell of baking bread fills the sanctuary during worship.
covenant	our promises as a nautical chart or map	"Come and Go With Me," *Singing the Journey* #1018, or "Take My Hand," a hymn by Jen Hazel in *Story, Song and Spirit*	Pack a bag with things that we need to take a journey, anticipating the items we'll want along the way. "Take My Hand," a hymn by Jen Hazel, in Story, Song and Spirit.
making mistakes	"We all spill soup"	"We All Spill Soup" by Mark Nepo in *The Book of Awakening* (entry for June 7)	"Accidentally" spill a bowl of brightly colored beads, shells, or seaglass (in an area where people won't need to walk during worship) and leave it messy for the rest of the service. (Appoint a post-worship clean-up helper in advance!)

A word of warning: Like pungent spices or chili peppers, metaphors are powerful. A little goes a long way. You don't need to name or repeat your central image in every worship component; nor do you have to be explicit. If you lay a trail of breadcrumbs throughout the service, weaving your metaphor through the different senses, people will enjoy following you all the way to the trail's end.

Finally, avoid puns. If metaphors are like chili peppers, puns are like anchovies: A few people really like them, but many people will groan and hold their noses at the first whiff.

In summary:

DO	DON'T
Center worship around an image or metaphor that can be engaged visually and through at least one other sense.	Rely on generic or abstract themes that will leave people confused, or that require wordy explanations.
Be subtle. People want to connect the dots by themselves.	Go over the top by including the metaphor in every single hymn and spoken worship component.
Find hymns that reflect the image by searching hymns and readings for key words.	Rely solely on the subject index or category listings in our hymnals.
Be playful.	Be punny.

Energy in the Transitions

It's possible that, as your sermon is incorporated into your congregation's worship calendar, you'll be invited or even encouraged to give input on the order of service. You and the program's leader should be respectfully aware of the decision-making structure —the network of responsibility and accountability—in your congregation. Who chooses hymns for worship, and how far in advance? Are they able to accommodate your requests for hymns that complement your sermon? Likewise, you may have an idea for a children's story that would be perfect for a Story for All Ages. In your congregation, does that liturgical piece "belong" to someone?

It may be an elaborate process to get answers to these questions, requiring time and conversations with people who aren't part of this program. By virtue of preparing and delivering a sermon, however, your shared ministry includes the role of worship leader. At this point in the program, you're developing the capacity to regard sermons as far more than a collection of words and ideas. As you wrestle with stories, images, theological reflection, and the voice in your sermon, it's time to consider one more aspect of preaching, the energy that flows—or gets stuck—as the sermon and the worship service unfold.

Worship is a vessel for the community and Spirit to visit one another; an energy fills that time and space. From its first moment to the last shared experience, a worship service is an arc through time. Each point of that arc has an energy; the emotion, pace, or volume shifts along the arc. You can feel big energy, or a spike in emotion, when a joyful hymn gets people moving, or when the congregation breaks into spontaneous and kind laughter. Big energy isn't necessarily loud, though—it's possible for charged, you-could-hear-a-pin-drop silence to have tremendous intensity.

Every service has its moments of small energy too—and this is as it should be. We need calm pockets of time in which to soften. Sometimes this includes singing hymns softly, meditatively, and seated. Slowing down or quieting the energy of a service is appropriate when the moment calls for reflection, mourning, or going inward.

One of the biggest mistakes that worship leaders make is failing to acknowledge that these energy shifts within the worship service are real, palpable, and malleable—especially in the transition between elements, such as moving from a prayer into a hymn. Some leaders, whether by design or accident, fashion worship services that are high energy from beginning to end—every moment marked by a hyped frenzy of emotion. Other services are flat from start to finish, like a bleak, horizontal landscape, where the eyes strain to catch a splash of color. Others still are marked by haphazard shifts in energy that leave people with energetic whiplash.

The vessel of worship is not constructed of unrelated segments. It's the worship leader's responsibility to stitch the components into a unified garment, to plan how the energy of worship will carry in the transitions—with the understanding that not everything goes according to plan in worship. For example, it's all too common for a quiet, meditative moment of silence or prayer to be shattered by a well-meaning worship leader springing up and loudly announcing the hymn. Abrupt transitions like this are unnecessary and disruptive.

As you pull together your sermon and the worship elements that will surround it in the service, think in terms of energy. Where does your sermon call for reading at a faster pace, a louder voice, or with stronger emotion? Where does your sermon beg for slowing down and quieting? Are there transitions within the sermon—perhaps a shift from a story to theological reflection—that you need to practice making differently?

Session 4

How have our experiences and our stories shaped our spirituality?

Snapshot

This session invites you to shift from personal story-telling and simple autobiography to theological reflection. You'll consider how your life experience intersects with your spiritual life and/or religious beliefs.

Chalice Pages   15 minutes

Reading the Covenant   5 minutes

Is there anything you want or need to add? Has every person been taking responsibility for upholding the promises you've made to each other?

Discussion of Reading F   10 minutes

- Which aspects of O'Neill's sermon were most effective or meaningful to you?
- What structure did you notice beneath the story?
- How did O'Neill's metaphor help you consider whether you're withholding something precious in your life?

What You'll Need

- a reflection (600–800 words)
- pen or pencil
- journal, notebook, or other place to write

Reading and Listening   75 minutes

- Did the reflection offer hope?
- Did you feel invited or challenged?
- How did the reflection engage your heart?
- What part of the reflection will you continue to think about?
- Is there any point at which the reader might be invited to remember any of the guidelines discussed in the last session?
- Where is there room for the reader to expand or elaborate?

Break   10 minutes

Reading and Listening   20 minutes

Group Reading: Theological Reflection   25 minutes

Our lives are built on, and from, stories. The world is made of stories. Throughout your work together, your reflections have contained stories that have shaped you.

Autobiographical sermons can be interesting, especially in smaller congregations where people are close friends. It's a heartwarming and even fascinating process to learn more about those we care about. However, today you will be focusing on taking sermons to a level deeper than autobiography.

At their best, sermons offer more than vivid stories, psychological analysis, and philosophical musings—they also provide spiritual or religious substance. This can be challenging for Unitarian Universalists because we tend to operate out of psychology rather than theology. It's also common for sermon writers to quote or cite one (or more) of our seven Unitarian Universalist Principles—and yet, collectively, our Principles lack theological language.

Ideally, your sermon will offer a snapshot of your Unitarian Universalist identity; it will reveal something about your religious or spiritual beliefs and how they were shaped. In other words, your sermon will contain theological reflection: your story, your life, your wisdom passed through the lens of your faith.

Here is a step-by-step theological reflection process for Unitarian Universalists:

Step	Example
Begin with your story. Choose a concrete, personal experience from your life and describe it (who, what, when, where).	During my college years, I was at the bank and saw a stack of brightly colored bills on the counter. "What country are those from?" I asked the teller. She looked at me curiously. "What are you talking about? Those are food stamps."
Describe some of the feelings that accompanied your experience.	I felt ashamed. I felt mortified. I had tried to have a conversation about international travel with the teller, but instead came face-to-face with my ignorance, not to mention my privilege. (Later, I felt grateful for my family and upbringing.)
Step back to the "balcony"—the big picture view—and address the following kinds of questions: What did I bring to this moment from my past? What cultural or spiritual beliefs were in play? What might psychology, family systems theory, or philosophy have to say about my experience?	I grew up in a middle-class family where, despite penny-pinching, there was always food on the table. My parents valued interacting with people of other cultures, so by college, I'd traveled to at least ten countries. I'd seen stark poverty and was somewhat aware of poor people in my own town, but could easily choose not to see them or wonder how they fed their own kids.
Review your experience in spiritual or religious terms. What spiritual opportunities exist(ed)? Wrestle with religious concepts such as right relationship, justice, inclusion, forgiveness, healing, and so on. Provide your own definitions for religious terms, if this seems appropriate.	I realized that *privilege* means not needing to see certain things, experience certain things, or even know about certain things. Even when we're wearing lenses that give specific shape and color to the way we see the world, we don't know it. On that day, my lenses led me to see exotic foreign currency in the place of a symbol of poverty—and up until that day, they had protected me from seeing what was right in front of me.

Step	Example
Elaborate on the "so what?" of your experience. How have you applied your learning to the rest of your journey? Has it informed or expanded your identity as a Unitarian Universalist? How did this experience change you and how will you be different?	That day in the bank forced me to acknowledge that my privilege grants me permission to not care about poverty —and to choose to care anyway. When I acknowledge that I—a straight, white, able-bodied, middle-class, graduate-degree-wielding woman—walk through the world differently than someone who's black, or gay, or Muslim, or disabled, or on food assistance, I am changed, and the world starts to change. When I use my own privilege to give voice or power to others, I change, and the world changes. When any of use our power in the service of freedom, the world changes.

What makes theological reflection different than simple story-telling? How does it feel to think about shaping your next written reflection according to this model?

Likes and Wishes   5 minutes

What did you appreciate about today's session? What would you like to see change?

Review of Preparation for Session 5

- Read through Session 5.
- Write a 1,200-word reflection to read out loud to the group. Incorporate theological reflection into your work.
- Read "The Answer I Wish I'd Given" (Reading I).
- Read "Theological Reflection Worksheet" (Reading J).
- Read "Stories Too Powerful to Tell" (Reading K).

Chalice Pages   15 minutes

The Answer I Wish I'd Given

I had jet-lag. That's my excuse—that, and it was a hot, humid Sunday afternoon in Chicago, the end of a three-day family reunion. All of us were well-fed and happy, but tired and . . . well, our family had been together for three days. When my aunt remembered that she needed to return the flower vases to her church, I volunteered to jump in the car with her and my mom.

To re-cap: I had jet-lag, it was hot, and I was enjoying the peace of a Sunday drive. That's how I got caught off-guard by a simple question.

As for how the question arose, I recall only that my aunt mentioned her church's mission and outreach programs. Recently, the church had sent a team of volunteers to New Orleans, where citizens were still cleaning up two years after Hurricane Katrina had mowed a path of destruction through it.

My aunt holds deeply conservative political values, which she holds in check under the best of circumstances. As I've already described, our weary afternoon was not the best of circumstances.

"That city has had two years to clean up and they're still asking for help," she huffed. "Tell me, Erika: Why should we help them?" There it was: the ball out of left field, the surprise attack on the right flank. Any way you look at it, I choked.

"Um," I said. Really: How do you begin to answer a question like that? We were talking about her church—and not just any church: It was the church that my mom and uncle attended as college students, the church where my parents held their wedding reception, the church where my cousin was married, the church where, as a teenager, I heard the best sermon about Jesus I've ever heard. But clearly, the answer had eluded her.

"They seem to think that they don't have to do anything," she continued, "except sit and wait for other people to come help them. How long do they expect us to keep helping?" (Notice how many *theys* she was up to.)

"Well," I fumbled, "When I lived there, we used to joke that New Orleans is the most developed of all the Third World nations. I mean, they operate under a different legal system. It was hard to work through the red tape when it was whole—now it's a city with broken hope and a broken infrastructure, so . . . ."

Lovely, isn't it, how I decided to explain the civic and legal framework of New Orleans, instead of answering my aunt's question? And, oh, friends, it gets worse. I proceeded to explain the quirks of land ownership and inheritance, for which my aunt had a counter-argument, until from the front seat Ma "Peacemaker" Hewitt wisely drew our attention to a new subject.

I was on vacation in Chicago that day, but apparently my personal angel was still at home. If she'd been on duty, she would have dope-smacked me (lovingly) before I'd uttered my first sentence; she'd have put three words in my mouth when it fell open, three little words that form the only possible answer to the question "Why should we help?"—the answer I wish I'd given: Because we can.

Because we can. We should help because we can. We share what we have with others because we can. That's the quick-and-dirty answer. Ever since that hot summer day, my aunt's question has been stuck to my frontal lobe like peanut butter sticks to your palate. That's why I want to take my answer a little further—and because I think we all ask a version of that question from time to time: Why do we give?

Take note: I hereby change my aunt's question from Why should we help them? to Why should we help? I'm uncomfortable with the notion of a *them*, because it means *they* are not part of *us*. As Unitarian Universalists, we believe in the interdependent web of all existence; our human family is woven from the same fabric. I happen to feel a connection to New Orleans because I've lived there, and people I love still live there. Whether suffering rains down on New Orleans or Myanmar, Knoxville or China, reaching outward in gestures of help is a means of reinforcing—of re-weaving—the frayed strands in our web of connection. Whom we help isn't as important as the fact of our helping.

That helps rid the question of the distasteful word *should*. The new question becomes Why do we have a responsibility to help others? Even better: Why are we called to give of ourselves? This question applies, conveniently, to any and all means of giving, whether it's to our congregation, to our Unitarian Universalist movement, or to someone in need.

The fact, however disquieting, is that giving often comes more easily when it's directed toward a crisis, or toward the collective (i.e., entire cities or countries) than toward a single stranger. When groups are in trouble (the victims of flooding, say, or political oppression), the need is evident; our help is triggered readily. On an individual basis, though, we risk second-guessing ourselves, our inner instinct to share lost in a flurry of suspicion and quiet judgment.

At the highway exit near my house, there's usually a panhandler at the light, holding a sign and a hopeful expression that burns right through my windshield. Is it right to roll down my window and give him one of the dollar bills that I keep in my ashtray? (If you're ever in my neck of the woods, it's a tan Corolla with "TRUST LV" plates. I don't always lock the doors. Help yourself.)

As a church pastor, I receive out-of-the-blue phone calls every so often from strangers who sing me their blues and recount terrible losses of luck. Am I called to take out

the checkbook for the Minister's Discretionary Fund—created by my congregation and entrusted to me—to ease their burdens for a night?

These aren't uncommon decisions. In her book *The Samaritan's Dilemma*, political scientist Deborah Stone parses a situation from her own life:

A few years ago . . . our local newspaper carried a story headlined "Panhandler Concerns Residents." It seems that every day, a man stood . . . holding a sign reading "Hungry." Many residents complained to the selectmen. . . . When the topic came up at the next selectmen's meeting, the chairman asked, "What are you going to do, arrest him and give him a meal?"

Sixty years ago, that would have been precisely the response to a hungry vagrant in small-town New Hampshire. He would have been taken to the jail if there was one, to an inn or a home if there wasn't, and there he'd be fed. Thirty years ago, a local official might even have helped him sign up for food stamps or welfare. But now, feeding a hungry man would seem to be trouble waiting to happen, for [another selectman] advised the townspeople, "The best way to avoid the problem is not to give out free food." . . .

To be sure, common morality still calls for feeding a hungry man, yet today, when I tell this story and ask audiences what they think the selectman meant, everyone seems to know. It's as if I'd asked a kindergarten class the color of the sky.

"If you give out free food, the man will just keep coming back for more."

"Other poor people will come to the town, knowing that there's free food."

"If you help him, you're just enabling him."

These answers pretty well summarize the new conventional wisdom: "Help is harmful. Think twice before you do it, and do it with restraint."

Aha, I think: There's the true chasm that my aunt and I were bickering across that day, the yawning gap between our two different poles of belief. She believes that help should be given judiciously to those in need, so as not to compound the problem—the "problem" being that, in her eyes, people ask for help when they don't really need it, or when they've grown dependent on the help of others.

I've worked in enough soup kitchens, mental health clinics, and Habitat for Humanity sites to believe something different: Most people ask for help only when they're so trapped by their need that they're willing to exchange a piece of their dignity by calling attention to it. I've come to believe that most people will ask for help only as long as they need it, and—moreover—that giving is helpful to both the recipient and the giver: In helping, in giving, we come to see and appreciate our own resources more deeply. There's a vast expanse between being responsible with our resources and fearfully hoarding what we have, attributing to others greed or laziness when their resources run thin.

Here's another way of defining our respective views of the world: My aunt's experience is funneled through scarcity metaphors: life is comprised of stockholders, "zero-sum games and pies with only so many slices"—a mentality Stone calls "mine-or-thine." In contrast (and on a day when my personal angels aren't off gallivanting somewhere else), I see life moving in metaphors of abundance, "continuity, circular flows, and widening ripples . . . mine-and-thine."

Why are we called to give of ourselves? When my car and I are idling at the exit ramp, it might be prudent to ask myself, "Is this guy really homeless? What will he do with this money? Does he really need help?" I'd hate to waste a dollar, after all—right? After careful consideration, it's a gamble I'm willing to take, more often than not. I would rather hand him a dollar bill than sit with the uncomfortable grain of knowledge that I looked away from someone declaring himself in need. What, after all, is the true cost of purposefully looking through, or past, someone who's asking for help? When I pretend not to see another human being, it exacts a steeper cost—a dram of my soul— than a measly dollar.

It should be evident to you by now how I respond when a red light pins me in front of a panhandler, or a stranger visits my office with a burden that needs to be eased. I use common sense; of course I do. I've called landlords to verify that someone is a day away from eviction, for example. But I do not examine homeless families for evidence of true poverty before paying for their motel room. Perhaps this is a Pollyanna-ish tack to take, this trust in strangers' integrity and their stories of need.

But giving is, for me, both a statement and expression of my faith. I give, in all the ways I give and from all the means that I can give, with intention. I give to strangers in need. I give to my congregation, with its mission to transform its members so that we may transform the world. I give to Unitarian Universalist organizations—such as the UU Service Committee and my District's Chalice Lighters program—so that my monetary statement of faith is amplified by merging with the gifts of others. I give because I choose not to harden my gaze and narrow my heart. I choose not to be seduced from my perch—where abundance is visible and alive in the world—by the siren song of "there's not enough . . . hang onto what's yours."

On most days—when my personal angel (my muse, my cerebral cortex, whatever) clocks in on time, alert and ready to guide me—I remember that I give because I can. For me, "I can" is a reflection that much of what I have, I did not earn. I've received freely from the generosity and privilege of others. What's "mine" isn't entirely mine, any more than the oxygen that flows through my lungs is mine. I wish for a portion of my

resources, along with my goodwill, to reverberate through the universe, doing good in as many ways as possible.

There are innumerable ways to name the forces that compel us to help others, all of them overlapping and none of them more important than the rest. You're a generous people: You have your own reasons for helping, for giving. Know them. Examine them. Practice articulating them.

Because here's the truth: It's not that my "angel" failed me on that humid Sunday in Chicago. I failed. I failed to speak, with the full conviction of my faith, and the bold power of my love for this crazy patchwork family of human beings to which we belong.

I didn't know how to answer my aunt's question on that long-ago summer afternoon. But I know the answer now. I'll never be caught off-guard again.

Theological Reflection Worksheet

This sermon-writing guide is based on the belief that every person has a profound truth to share, and that we each live in service to it. Your truth is more than just a cognitive belief—it's a lived experience. As explained in the group reading in Session 4, "Theological Reflection," there are often spiritual truths and wisdom attached to our everyday stories. The chart in that reading provides an example of how to connect one to the other.

This worksheet will walk you more thoroughly through the steps of theological reflection, which is part of the Christian tradition, especially in Roman Catholicism. A version of the process described in this book was taught for years to seminary students by Rosemary Chinnici, retired professor of pastoral theology at Starr King School for the Ministry. She, in turn, adapted the process from the book *Method in Ministry: Theological Reflection* by James D. and Evelyn Eaton Whitehead.

Note: Introverts have an easier time reflecting silently and by themselves, while extraverts often need to talk out loud in order to discover what they think. If you're an extravert, you might find a buddy to walk through this exercise with verbally, almost as though you're interviewing each other.

First Step: The Facts

Begin with a personal story from a reflection that you've already read aloud to the group. In a few lines, summarize that story. Who was involved? Is the timing significant? The place?

If your written reflections haven't yet included a personal story, back up by beginning with a statement of belief or conviction that has shown up in one of your reflections. In a few sentences, describe an incident that helped you form this belief.

Second Step: The Feelings

Elaborate by describing your feelings—a step that could be more complex than it sounds. Rev. Abigail Johnson, a minister in the United Church of Canada, suggests, "Asking ourselves what challenged, stimulated, or disturbed us is another way to get at the question of feelings." Keep your feeling-statements short and simple, and start with "I," as in "I felt lonely" or "I felt connected." Stick to feelings for now. Johnson reminds us, "As soon as you add other words, then you are moving into thinking rather than feeling. For example, 'I feel that . . . .' shifts away from what you are feeling into statements and opinions."

Third Step: The Balcony

Explore the context of the story. At the time of that experience, who were you? How would you describe your identity, either at the time or now? What values did you bring to it? Did your feelings affect your behavior or choices? If so, how? Try to distinguish between what you understood at the time and what you understand today about that experience.

Fourth Step: The Spiritual

In this story-telling, it may become evident which of your current beliefs are core beliefs—in other words, what's of utmost importance to you. You might discover something that serves as your "Ultimate Reality," as theologian Paul Tillich called it. These convictions may have little or nothing to do with a being some call God, but may point to Mystery or to That Which Is Larger Than Us.

As you delve one more layer deeper into your story, ask yourself, In what parts of the story do any of these religious or spiritual concepts become apparent? Where does the story reveal some part of your credo—saying, "This I believe"?

This step might be an opportunity for you to reclaim and/or redefine a word that's been problematic for you, such as *God* or *prayer*. It might be a chance to plumb, from a spiritual angle, words that are both theological and secular, such as *forgiveness* or *justice*. Or you might find yourself taking a neutral term such as *whole* and providing a richly textured spiritual framework around it.

As mentioned in Session 4, do your best to avoid listing or quoting our Unitarian Universalist Principles in your reflection—because first and foremost the purpose of this process is to express a belief in your own words. If one of the Principles speaks to you, see whether you can describe it in a new way.

Secondly, as Rev. Douglas Taylor notes, "the Principles are not theology, but there is theology behind them." The Principles don't explicitly present theological claims, but they reflect aspects of Unitarian Universalist theology. For example, the first Principle reflects our theology of human nature, and the fourth lifts up our epistemology—"how we know what we know," the source of our authority. If your sermon includes Principles, try investigating the beliefs underneath them.

Fifth Step: Bring It Home

Most theological reflection cycles conclude with praxis. This is the embodiment—the lived experience—of what we've learned. It's what we do with our reflections, how we're changed or inspired to live differently.

You've described the facts of a story, and the feelings that accompanied it. You've employed a bird's-eye view of who you were in that situation—how you came to be that person, with those beliefs and behaviors. You've also drawn from spiritual or religious language to make sense of that incident today and to provide it with theological texture.

In this final step, describe the "so what?" of the experience. What's the relationship between this event and your being a Unitarian Universalist? Who are you today as a person of faith because of the event? How have your relationships been affected?

Also, remember that your sermon will be delivered to other Unitarian Universalists. How might this story invite them to embody your shared faith in a new way?

Stories Too Powerful to Tell

When you choose a story from your life to include in your sermon, you may find your-self exploring the often-blurry line between vulnerability and oversharing.

Some stories are gloriously powerful because they force us to risk looking less than perfect, and that vulnerability creates—in us and those who hear it—an opening for grace or healing to occur. Stories are particularly rich fodder for a sermon when they reveal something new about us, encourage a new layer of faith or identity to form, and are personal enough to let listeners drop their guard and follow us to a more tender place.

Other stories, however, are too powerful to tell in public; they are so personal that they're more appropriately kept private. These narratives are more suited for sharing with a covenant group or a lay pastoral associate than from the pulpit. Stories of a personal nature have profound ripple effects, both for us and for those who hear them from the pulpit.

Consider, first, your own self. Once you tell your story, you can't un-tell it. Would you feel comfortable if your story found its way to members of your family? Your co-workers, your ex-spouse, your neighbors? Given our wired society, your sermon can eas-ily reach the ears or eyes of someone you didn't expect. (Note that congregations should always ask permission before posting mp3 or digital versions of your sermons on their websites.) Ask yourself whether you'd be willing to hand out copies of your story at your local coffee shop. If not, then reassess whether to preach about it.

Next, there's a reality that ministers bear in mind Sunday after Sunday: We don't always know who our listeners are at their core. Even after years of knowing someone, we can't know their secret struggles or the ghosts in their past. For example, people who have survived trauma—such as sexual abuse or battering—can experience re-trauma-tization, experiencing flashes of panic or fear when they hear an in-depth account of a similar experience. People who have been affected by violence still bear unconscious tripwires which, if triggered, can send their whole being back into fearfulness. Needless to say, this shouldn't happen in worship. As another example, if you tell a story about witnessing someone kill an animal, some of your listeners may feel distraught while others may experience genuine trauma, requiring support and counseling from your minister or other mental health professionals in the days and weeks to come. If you're not sure whether you should include a particular story in your sermon, you might ask your minister or a worship associate about how the story could affect the congregation.

In addition, remember that children and teens may be present when you preach. Is your story appropriate for them? Would it be wise to publicize your sermon as "including issues of an adult nature"? Some stories—while profound and life-changing to you—will take a toll on some of your listeners. This is not the kind of power you want to wield in the pulpit. Try to find a story that captures your experience in a more life-giving way.

Be brave, but be wise.

Session 5

How do we turn our stories into theological reflection?

Snapshot

From this point forward, you'll continue to develop your theological reflection skills in your sermon preparation. This session also focuses on strengthening trust and connection as you move toward delivering a final sermon.

Chalice Pages   15 minutes

Reading the Covenant   5 minutes

Reading and Listening   60–70 minutes

- Does the reflection go beyond storytelling or autobiography?
- Does the reflection include analysis from a larger perspective (the balcony view)?
- What about the reader's experience expanded their religious tradition?
- What about the reader's religious life helps them understand their experience?
- How has the reader's experience changed them? How are they different as a result?

Break   10 minutes

> ### What You'll Need
> - a 1,200-word reflection
> - a pen or pencil
> - a journal, notebook, or other place to write

Reading and Listening   60–70 minutes

Debriefing   5 minutes

How is the process of reading and providing feedback serving you? How might you even further deepen the trust and comfort level in the group?

Looking Ahead   5 minutes

Likes and Wishes   5 minutes

What did you appreciate about today's session? What would you like to see change?

Review of Preparation for Session 6

- Read through Session 6.
- Write a 1,500-word sermon to read out loud to the group. Whether you keep kneading a reflection that you've already read or decide to tackle a new subject, be aware that the next session will be your last one before your group begins reading completed sermons.
- Think about the images or metaphors that are emerging in your sermon. If applicable, reflect on which readings or hymns in a worship service might reflect and strengthen these images or metaphors.

Chalice Pages   15 minutes

Session 6

What have you discovered in yourself and in one another?

Snapshot

This is the last regular session before you present full-length sermons. As such, it's devoted entirely to the process of reading, listening, and providing feedback. (Please note: the times suggested for this session assume that there are eight participants in your group, and that all of them will read their sermons at this gathering.)

Chalice Pages   10 minutes

Reading the Covenant   5 minutes

Looking Ahead   5 minutes

Standing in the Pulpit

For a smooth transition to the pulpit:

- Print your sermon in a clear font and in large print—18-point or larger. Reading from large text will take more paper (you can re-use paper, printing on the back, if it disturbs you to use so much paper), but it will also help you to look up from your manuscript and then find your place easily when you look back down.

What You'll Need

- a 1,500-word sermon
- a pen or pencil
- a journal, notebook, or other place to write

- Create 3-inch margins at the bottom of each page so that at the end of each page your chin doesn't drop, and deaden your voice. Many people make the mistake of creating small margins in order to save paper, but when they reach the bottom of the page, the microphone can end up near their forehead.
- Number your pages clearly. If they happen to fall on the floor, you'll be spared a long and uncomfortable re-ordering process.
- When you speak into a microphone, your voice will sound loud to your own ears. It should—it will need to travel to the very back of the sanctuary and be heard by those who have trouble hearing.
- If you normally wear glasses or bifocals, bring them with you to the pulpit. You may not know ahead of time whether you'll need them.
- When you practice reading your sermon out loud at home, practice it standing up (or otherwise in the position from which you plan to deliver it). Notice what it's like to speak, without leaning or shifting, for nearly twenty minutes. Identify what your body needs in order to feel comfortable and at ease for such a long time.

Reading and Listening   65 minutes

After so much practice listening one another into wise writing, use your own experience to guide this listening process.

Break   5 minutes

Reading and Listening   70 minutes

Likes and Wishes   10 minutes

What did you appreciate about today's session? What would you like to see change?

Knowing that this is your last session in this format, how would you like to celebrate and acknowledge the end of this program?

Review of Preparation for Sessions 7 and 8

- Read through Sessions 7 and 8.

- Have your sermon—or the most complete version possible—ready to read on the day you signed up for.
- Re-read "Standing in the Pulpit," the group reading from this session.

Chalice Pages   10 minutes

Sessions 7 and 8

Listening, preaching, and affirming

Snapshot

Over the course of your last two sessions, you'll have an opportunity to preach a full-length sermon from your congregation's pulpit. One focus of your energy will be integrating your reading with all of the physical adjustments that the pulpit demands from preachers. These sessions also celebrate all the hard work and reflection that you've put into the program!

(Please note: the times suggested for these sessions assume that there are eight participants in your group, and that half of them will read their sermons at each gathering.)

Preparing to Listen   15 minutes

It's time! After weeks (or months) of forming connections and exploring your own creative spirit, these final two sessions represent a completion of sorts. Most participants find themselves polishing and tweaking their sermon right up until the morning of its delivery, so the sermon you read today may simply be "as complete as possible."

Before your sermon-reading begins, gather as a group to hold a few moments of silence together, light a chalice, or otherwise mark your stepping into a sacred time and space as friends who have shared this journey together. It's also recommended that you decide, as a group or with the leader's input, how it will be handled if anyone's sermon goes over twenty minutes.

Your listening and feedback will feel different in this session. You should be gathering in your sanctuary or meeting house, which adds some new elements to the process

> **What You'll Need:**
> - your sermon, if it's your day to read
> - a pen or pencil
> - a journal, notebook, or other place to write

of reading—such as the sound system and the demands on your body as you stand to read (as you are able). As listeners, scatter yourselves in the seats or pews so that the preacher can learn how to shift their gaze throughout the space.

As you listen with your wise heart to each sermon, also consider these technical questions:

- Can you hear the person clearly?
- If not, is it due to the sound system, or does the speaker seem reluctant to speak loudly?
- Is the speaker's body language distracting?

Preaching and Listening   60 minutes

Half of those who are reading today will do so before the break. Each sermon should be no longer than twenty minutes, and there may be time for up to ten minutes of feedback if there are four readers in this session (two before the break, two after).

Following each sermon, observe one minute of silence. But then, before gathering in the front of the sanctuary to share feedback—and if it feels natural—why not offer the speaker some rousing applause? The speaker just did a wonderful thing, and it took tremendous energy, time, and courage. Bravo!

Break   10 minutes

Preaching and Listening   60 minutes

Continue with the process of having designated participants preach their sermon, sit for a minute of silence, receive applause from the group, and receive feedback.

Closing   15 minutes

Share general affirmations or responses to the process of listening to each other deliver sermons from the pulpit. Gather together again in a circle and share silence, a song familiar to the congregation, or a group hug (or all three!).

Ending the Program

If your group chooses to share a meal, or to otherwise gather for a celebration of all that you've learned and shared together, you might use the following as a means of creating closure.

Whoever shows up are the right people
Whatever happens is what needs to happen
Whenever it starts (or happens) is the right time
Be open to God, whose middle name is Surprise
When it's over, it's over
  —Center for Pastoral Effectiveness

*   Given your experience in this group, do any (or all) of these guiding principles resonate as true for you?
*   What do you think is meant by the last one, When it's over, it's over?
*   What does it mean for this program to be "over," even though you might not preach your sermon for quite some time?
*   What will its being "over" mean for the relationships that have been created among you?

A Final Wish

By opening this book and looking into the terrain of this program, you spread out a map of courage and creativity in front of you. Where did you stumble? Where did you discover new wonders? Is there any moment along this journey that deepened your spiritual life or shifted your conviction? What will you carry with you, now that this program has ended?

Whatever questions you discovered, may you continue to wrestle with them until they bless you.

Whatever friendships and connections were born, may those relationships continue to deepen in trust and love.

Whatever wisdom you've mined, may it enrich the next leg of the journey.

As you keep bringing your gifts and yourself to shared ministry, never forget that you minister through who you are. May you live more abundantly, more generously, and more boldly for what you've shared here.

Leader's Notes

By taking on the role of program leader, you're doing a grand and beautiful thing. It's no easy feat to be a vision-caster, a time-keeper, a meeting-organizer, and a cheerleader, but you'll surely find ease in the role—and cooperation from participants—as the program unfolds.

This chapter contains some theory and logistics to consider before your program gets off the ground. As the leader, some of your logistical responsibilities require you to:

- publicize the program, either recruiting or inviting participants from your congregation. Even if you as leader decide to invite specific people to join the group, publicizing your plans might create curiosity and support among the congregation's members
- explain the scope of the program, including its timing and parameters, to all participants *before* the first session
- provide set-up materials at sessions
- serve as facilitator for all sessions, which includes the delicate and tricky art of time-management
- provide reminders about meeting times
- if applicable, serve as liaison between the participants and the minister and/or Worship/Sunday Service Committee, to schedule sermons.

On a more abstract level, you'll likely discover that you need to invite people out of their heads and into their hearts. Sermon writing is not an academic enterprise; it falls far beyond the intellectual realm. You will need to consider how to encourage participants' trust in you and in the process. You'll also likely need to remind them that covenant and caring form the container for this spiritual growth.

How to Select Participants

This program can serve people of all ages, from youth or young adults to elders. Six to eight participants is ideal. Having more than eight means that at least one person will not get adequate reading and response time. It's up to you to decide whether to actively recruit—inviting potential participants on an individual basis—or to openly invite all who are interested.

Every time I lead this group, I employ both approaches. I call a handful of members whom I suspect to be hiding their light under a bushel and would blossom into leadership if given the opportunity. Some of them are eager to try on the role of preacher, while others agree reluctantly to be recruited, asking me to promise that they don't have to present a sermon if they don't want to (I always agree to these terms). I also put an open invitation in the newsletter about two months in advance, inviting people to contact me if they're interested or would like to know more about the program.

When discussing this program with potential participants:

- Emphasize that this isn't so much a group for writers as it is a small group ministry to invite spiritual and theological reflection. It matters not whether participants consider themselves to be writers. What matters is whether they're able to access their inner landscapes, mine them for their own unique wisdom, and make themselves vulnerable in sharing that with others.
- Clarify that sessions will be three hours long and will be held every two to three weeks.
- Go over the schedule of sessions with people, individually or as a group, so that there are no surprises as the program unfolds. As much as possible, do this scheduling *before* the group meets, as this task can become complicated if left until the first session. The best strategy is to first identify a good day of the week and meeting time—for example, Monday nights at 6:00—and then, as a second step, to choose which eight Monday nights will work best for the group.
- Ask each participant to bring a special notebook or folder to every session, for writing their Chalice Pages and other notes.
- Ask each participant to bring their datebook or family calendar to the first session.

I have found that nearly every participant emerges with a strong, suitable sermon to present to the congregation. On the rare occasion when someone's sermon isn't quite ready, the writer knows it and will not allow themselves to be scheduled on the worship calendar. It's always possible, however, that a participant's enthusiasm—or hubris—will far outpace their skills. This could be a very uncomfortable situation. As loving congregations, we wish to value and respect every person, and show our affirmation of them by accepting them—and their sermons—as less than perfect. On the other hand, this program is designed to create compelling, meaningful sermons so that the quality of worship doesn't suffer when the minister is out of the pulpit (if your congregation has a minister). Each congregation's leadership will weigh this balance in their own way, but as the leader of this program, you may find yourself in the delicate position of gate-keeper—letting the minister and/or Worship/Sunday Service Committee know which, if any, sermons need to incubate in a revision process before being scheduled.

Make Sessions Count

This program is founded on a few core commitments. They are listed below, with an explanation of why and how they make the program a transformative spiritual experience, and how you might shape them for your particular group.

You may be tempted to dismiss these commitments or allow participants to mutiny against them. Your participants will likely protest—especially the first time this is offered in your congregation—that they can't or don't want to honor one or more of these practices. Having led this program multiple times with dozens of UU laypeople, I can attest that by the end of the program every participant—including people who initially argued—expressed appreciation for the way the sessions were outlined, and believe that it would not have been as fulfilling otherwise.

Sessions Last for Three Hours . . . .

Some participants will balk at the notion of spending three whole hours in a session. They'll argue that it doesn't leave them time to eat dinner, or that they'll have to rush from work, or that they'd rather meet more often for two hours at a time.

The connecting, bonding, sermon-crafting business of this program is deep work. It will likely demand a more intense sharing and listening than any congregational program the participants have been involved in before. Please take this claim as a leap of faith if it's hard to believe: Unless your group has fewer than five participants, the deep work of this program can't fit into two-hour sessions.

I've found that the best meeting time is 6:00 to 9:00 on a weeknight. I encourage my "seminarians" to bring their dinner or snacks, if necessary, but ask them to wait to eat until after the Chalice Pages time is over.

. . . And Are Spaced Several Weeks Apart

It's helpful to space the eight sessions two or three weeks apart, with the exception of the last two sessions—when participants preach their sermons—which can be scheduled on back-to-back weeks. As the program unfolds, participants will appreciate having a few weeks in between sessions for them to develop their writing.

In my congregation, we held our first session in late May, after the group had chosen a day of the week and time to gather—Thursday nights, for example. Before the first session, I asked people to let me know about their vacations and other absences and patched together a summer schedule of Thursday night sessions. The last two sessions—when participants preached—fell around Labor Day weekend.

Each Session Begins and Ends with Chalice Pages

Many Unitarian Universalists are accustomed to beginning sessions with a check-in or some other way of sharing the high and low points of their week. Some have no other place to process the sorrows or anxieties of their day-to-day life, and even committee meetings can provide the kind of pastoral support that congregants hunger for.

While check-in can be valuable, it can also form a kind of verbal laundry pile in the center of the room, growing larger than intended as each person heaps on their contribution until the purpose of the meeting gets eclipsed by personal sharing.

This sermon program is based on the assumption that everyone has an important part of themselves to share and that their life experiences can shape the spiritual journeys of other people. Because the vehicle for that sharing is written, sessions begin with Chalice Pages—fifteen minutes of silent journal-writing—to form a cushion between the world and the intimate, soul-deep work of reading and listening to people's writing. Group participants who are uncomfortable with silence may request music during Chalice Pages. You might choose to turn that decision over to the group or you might feel that music—and the inevitable questions of who chooses it and how it's played—will distract from the writing.

The Group Forms and Shares a Covenant

When I lead this program in my congregation, I ask participants to make three promises —not just to me, but to each other. First, to make every possible effort to attend our sessions. Early on, it usually becomes clear that several people's jobs or vacations will take them away from a session, which is inevitable. (If I have to miss a session myself, I ask a graduate of the program in advance to lead that session.) Aside from our vacations and work trips, however, many people lead full and tiring lives. I ask people to commit up front to being present for their fellow group members. This is how I put it: "If you're tired, having a hard time leaving the house, and tempted to stay on the couch to watch TV, please promise us as a group that you'll get yourself in your car and join us anyway." In any case, many participants find that there's a magic that happens within the first few sessions—they need to be with the group because of how it fills their hearts.

The second promise I ask of my sermon-writers is part of a larger discussion of how our congregation's worship leaders plan and lead worship. The Worship Committee is comprised of trained worship associates who lead services in the minister's absence and are skilled at working collaboratively with guest ministers and speakers. During the course of the sermon seminar, I ask participants to pledge that, when their sermons are done and they feel confident scheduling a date to preach, each of them will work with a worship associate. As part of that process, the speakers can help plan the service and choose its elements—such as hymns or readings—and the worship associate or minister leads the service.

Finally, some people will be intrigued by the program but will feel understandably anxious about writing a sermon or delivering it in front of the congregation. I promise the group that no one will be forced to deliver a sermon—it is entirely their choice, as long as their participation is in good faith. I ask them to promise in return that they will trust the process and wait to see what emerges from their writing.

In addition to these three informal promises between us, the members of the group invite and sustain deep trust by forming a covenant, a set of promises and expectations for how they will be in relationship together. ("Development of Covenant" on pages 95–96 explains the process more fully.) The implication of all of these agreements is that each person is accountable and everyone present is responsible for the shared covenant.

Follow Reading with Silence

Sessions 2 through 6 center around participants reading their reflections out loud to the group and then receiving feedback. At the beginning of the program, individual reflections are on the brief side (200–300 words). As the program continues, reflections grow longer (700–900 words). Each reading is followed by a time for providing verbal and written feedback in accordance with the group's covenant.

Before the group offers feedback, however, everyone observes one minute of silence. This buffer between listening and responding has a power all its own. It provides some practical benefits, such as allowing people to write down their feedback and gather their thoughts. It also allows the energy to shift and the speaker to experience the power of letting their words linger in the air. Finally, the minute of silence counters our natural instinct to offer reactive praise. After all, after a sermon is preached in worship, there is no rushing to fill the space with exclamations of "That was great!"

A simple way to facilitate this silence is to allow a minute (or so) to pass after the reader has read, and then end the silence by thanking the reader.

Be Fair Timekeepers

As incredible as it might seem, the three hours of your session time will speed by—especially when the readings grow longer. Once your group becomes comfortable offering feedback in response to reflections, that time will seem preciously brief. You'll be surprised by the richness of people's writing and by how much feedback participants will have. In order to be fair to everyone, you will need to monitor the time limits in each session assiduously.

One way for everyone to take responsibility for honoring the time limit is by specifying the word count for each reflection. As a general rule, 100 words on paper takes about 1 minute to read out loud. In congregations where sermons are typically 20 minutes long, 2,200 words is the suggested maximum word count. If your congregation is suited to 15-minute sermons, then consider 1,700 words a reasonable ceiling. Participants who have trouble limiting their words will likely argue that it's possible to read more quickly so that their sermons can be longer than 2,200 (or 1,600) words. While it's true that it's possible to read that quickly, it's very difficult for listeners to hear and to process more than 100 words per minute. Sermons should be heard, taken in, and thoughtfully digested.

The Larger Worship Context

As mentioned in the chapter "The Worship Vessel," on page 1, it's helpful to consider the sermon within the context of the larger worship service. It wouldn't make sense to plant a garden without knowing something about the local soil and climate, or to sew a garment before you know who will be wearing it. Similarly, the sermons that emerge from this program will be more meaningful and effective if participants can help select other elements of the service. As mentioned in the essay "Images and Metaphors" (Reading G) on page 51, if a sermon centers around a certain image, that image might be echoed in hymns or readings throughout the service, or even in the message for all ages.

Depending on your congregation's structure, leadership, and respective understandings of whose turf is whose, this might be simple. If you, the program leader, are also the congregation's minister or a worship associate, it's likely that you're already willing and able to invite participants to share in worship planning. Take advantage of this chance to empower laypeople: Give them further confidence and freedom, which will translate into a deeper understanding of all that goes into planning excellent worship. Remember that, when our congregation's members practice working together as a team—for instance, with the musicians or the director of religious education—it strengthens congregational life.

On the other hand, it's also possible that including this program's participants in the larger worship planning of your congregation will be a delicate or downright problematic enterprise. For example, the music director may have established a vision and schedule for the music in upcoming worship and can't alter those plans without pulling the rest of the year askew. Or the accompanist might be a part-time contractor with little or no interest in fielding requests that would require extra work or preparation. There are any number of reasons—some of them entirely reasonable—why involving program participants in worship planning would be thorny.

Explore turf issues and process thoughtfully and in a timely manner, perhaps even before your first session. Remember that our congregations are based on relationship—and one of the central, ever-shifting dances of relationship is finding the balance of power, responsibility, and inclusion.

What the Leader Provides

- chalice
- chime or bell
- program schedule
- purpose statement from your congregation's worship/Sunday service committee (if applicable)
- markers (optional)
- easel and newsprint (optional)

Welcome   5 minutes

Welcome participants into the space, ask them to silence their phones, and invite them to introduce themselves by name.

Chalice Pages   15 minutes

Ask participants to take out paper and a pen—even if they've brought their laptops—and explain that the session will begin with silent writing time. If they have questions about the program, invite them to include these questions as part of their writing. If they're processing something that happened to them earlier in the day, suggest that they write about that. If they don't know what to write, invite them to start by saying so on the page—"I don't know what to write"—and see what emerges! Tell the group that when they see you light the chalice, they'll have one minute to finish any stray thoughts and put their pens down. After fourteen minutes, light the chalice.

leader's notes

91

Introductions and Overview   15 minutes

During the introductions, ask people to go around the circle to answer the question "What brought you here?"

Note: Some people may have questions to ask about the program. Assure them that there will be time later in the session for raising questions and concerns. Make careful note of those who do have something to raise by writing their names and topics in a Loose Ends list that will be addressed at the end of the session. You can also address some of those questions in the Expectations portion of the session.

Group Reading: What If?   5 minutes

As a group, read this selection aloud. Go around the circle as each person reads a line. Anyone can pass, if they choose.

Lightning Interviews   10 minutes

The name of this exercise reflects how briefly people will speak to each other while in pairs—one minute. Participants will pair up five times (each time the pairs should be different), and each pair will take turns sharing their answers to one of the provided questions. Their responses will not be shared with the group; this is simply a way for participants to become more familiar with one another. Some people will need to move around the room, while others who prefer or need to remain seated can do so. As the leader, it's easier for you to serve as timekeeper if you abstain from this activity. If there's an odd number of participants, have the group break into pairs plus one group of three.

Ask people to find their first partner and decide which one of the pair will respond to the question first. After thirty seconds, ring the chime or bell and invite the second person in the pair to answer the question. At the end of another thirty seconds, ring the bell or chime and announce that it's time for everyone to find a new partner.

For each of the questions, make sure that everyone is paired with someone new. Follow the same process with each question.

Expectations   10 minutes

Participants should experience few, if any, surprises. Review the basic outline and expectations for the program. Ask people to take out their calendars to confirm that they all have the next seven meeting dates scheduled. You can also address other questions at this time, or defer them to the time at the end of the session when you'll go over the Loose Ends list.

Discussion: What Is a Sermon?   30 minutes

Facilitate a conversation about the questions in the session plan for about fifteen minutes, making sure that everyone has a chance to share. A good rule of thumb is that nobody speaks a second time until everyone has spoken once, or has had the opportunity to speak and passed. It may be helpful to record the group's contributions on the newsprint for all to see, especially if comments fall into the contrasting categories of "sermon" and "not a sermon."

Ask participants to remain silent as they complete the sentence "At its most effective, a sermon makes me feel . . . ." After a couple minutes, invite them to go around the circle and read their responses out loud (as always, anyone may pass).

As you continue to facilitate the discussion, be aware that people naturally tend to find problems rather than offer affirmation. If participants begin to describe what made particular sermons meaningless or dull, gently repeat the questions: "Which sermons do you remember as being the most moving or meaningful? What makes a sermon memorable and meaningful to you?"

Allow responses to continue for up to ten minutes. Then ask people to reflect on what they've heard and, if applicable, what's been recorded on the newsprint.

Thank people for their thoughts and contributions, and invite them to stretch their legs for a ten-minute break.

Break   10 minutes

Discussion: Worship Authority in the Congregation   15 minutes

Lead a discussion around the questions in the session plan about where the spheres of responsibility and accountability overlap in the congregation's worship life. You—or a designated scribe—might make notes on newsprint to highlight the key points.

Share the sample Worship Committee purpose statement in the session plan and the purpose statement and/or covenant from your congregation's Worship or Sunday Service Committee. Continue the discussion by answering as a group the questions following the purpose statement in the session plan.

Group Reading: Authority in the UU Pulpit   25 minutes

Ask participants to read out loud, going around the circle, "Authority in the UU Pulpit," which is provided in the session plan. Lead a discussion around the questions that follow the reading.

Review of Preparation for Session 2

As a group, go over the preparation for Session 2, listed in the session plan, and answer any questions. If participants are interested in reading more on their own, suggest the chapter "Worthy Nonetheless: Ministerial Authority and Presence," in *Thematic Preaching* by Jane Rzepka and Ken Sawyer (2001, Chalice Press), pp. 195–201.

By now, your group might have already decided on dates and times for sessions 7 and 8 of this program (in which participants read their full sermons out loud from the pulpit). Remember to reserve the sanctuary or meetinghouse for those times as far in advance as necessary, avoiding potential conflicts over the space.

Visit the Loose Ends List   5 minutes

If there are any unanswered questions or concerns that haven't yet been addressed, address them now. If a question seems beyond the scope of the group—for example, "There were no paper towels in the restroom"—you may defer the issue until after the session, or promise an offline conversation with the participant at a later time.

Likes and Wishes   10 minutes

Facilitate a discussion in which the group provides both positive and constructive feedback about this session, based on the questions in the session plan.

Chalice Pages   15 minutes

Invite participants to begin writing in silence for about fifteen minutes. Explain that, when they see you extinguish the chalice, they'll have a minute or so to finish their thoughts and close their notebooks. After fourteen minutes, extinguish the chalice.

What the Leader Provides

- chalice
- timer
- index cards or paper
- sample haiku (optional)
- easel and newsprint (optional)
- markers (optional)

Chalice Pages   15 minutes

Welcome people and remind them that the first fifteen minutes will be spent writing in silence. Suggest that for this session they use a portion of the time to write a haiku, using the template in the session plan. If you wish, read aloud a sample haiku. After fourteen minutes, light the chalice to signal that they have one minute to finish any stray thoughts and put their pens down.

Reading of Haiku   5 minutes

Ask if anyone is willing to share their voice in the form of the haiku they wrote. Anyone may pass.

Development of Covenant   20 minutes

Ask the group to take a minute to reflect in their notebooks about what they need from each other, using the questions in the session plan as a guide.

Invite people to share their contributions to the covenant. As they do so, act as scribe, recording their responses on newsprint or in a notebook (or you can invite a volunteer to do this). Participants will likely offer ideas that fall into two categories: a larger covenant of care and respect, and specific practices for giving and receiving feedback. It might be helpful to create a section of the covenant that specifically addresses questions like "When we share our writing, how do we wish to give and receive feedback?" and "Will the content of our reflections be confidential?"

Once your draft covenant is written down—perhaps organized into two sections—read it together. Type it up or ask your scribe to do so and give it to participants before or at Session 3. You don't need to consider it a completed document; as a group, you'll revisit the covenant at the beginning of every session, making changes if necessary.

Reading and Listening 80 minutes

Pass out index cards or paper, or ask participants to take out their own paper to write down feedback for each reader. (Dissuade people from tearing off tiny scraps of paper, which suggests that they'll have little in the way of feedback.) Tell them that they will listen to each other read their reflections and offer verbal feedback, but there will not be time for every listener to provide verbal feedback so they should also write down their notes for the reader. Ask participants to hold the questions from the session plan in their minds as they listen and write their notes for the person who's reading.

Each reflection of 200–300 words should take three minutes to read out loud, with one minute of silence to follow. If there are eight people ready to read, feedback after each reflection will need to be limited to six minutes. If six people read, feedback can last longer. Do your best, as timekeeper, to provide the same amount of time to each reader in the given time period of eighty minutes. If these calculations make you twitchy, let mathematically gifted group members help.

Remind the group that readers might be feeling vulnerable. This is more a spiritual exercise than an editorial one. The group's job is not to correct grammar but to strengthen the reader's ability to trust their voice. Participants should ask themselves how their feedback will make the reader stronger, more confident, or glad that they shared out loud.

As people begin to read, the group will instinctively want to offer praise as soon as the reader finishes. You may need to offer a gentle reminder that each reading is followed by a minute of silence.

At the end of each feedback period, remind listeners to give their feedback cards or paper to the person who's just read. You might also field questions or comments, choosing to address them before the break, or postpone addressing them until the end of the session. Remind participants to give their feedback cards or paper to each other. You might also field questions or comments, choosing to address them before the break, or postpone addressing them until the end of the session.

When the readings end, ask the group whether it was difficult to hold silence for one minute, and to reflect on how deep, honest sharing can release palpable energy in a space. At times, silence provokes anxiety. Ask people how they experience the energy in the room. What does it feel like—for both the reader and the listeners?

Break   15 minutes

Give people a chance to stretch their legs, visit the restroom, or otherwise take care of themselves.

Debriefing   5 minutes

Invite group members to share their responses to the question in the session plan, or the following questions: Did the reading and listening activity connect to the group's covenant? What, if anything, made readers feel more confident? If necessary, revisit or make changes to the listening/feedback section of the group covenant.

Discussion: Who's Preaching?   15 minutes

Remind the group that the main focus of this session is that a sermon isn't about how much you know, or even what you know—it's about who you are. Who are you? What does your voice sound like?

Ask them to discuss the questions in the session plan.

Group Reading: Sermon Structure   15 minutes

Tell the group that, in years past, the UUA awarded a prestigious prize called the Borden Sermon Award. Applicants submitted sermons that followed the steps described in Richard C. Borden's book *Public Speaking—As Listeners Like It!* Explain that, while there are many valid and interesting ways to organize sermons, the four steps that Borden proposed are one straightforward way to think about structuring them.

Ask for volunteers to read each step out loud, adapted from Borden's book and listed in the session plan.

Discuss other ways to structure a sermon.

Likes and Wishes   5 minutes

Facilitate a discussion in which the group provides both positive and constructive feedback about this session, based on the questions in the session plan.

Review of Preparation for Session 3

As a group, go over the preparation for Session 3, listed in the session plan, and answer any questions. Before your next session, circulate the first draft of the group's covenant.

Chalice Pages   15 minutes

Invite the group to write in silence. Extinguish the chalice after fourteen minutes to signal that the session has ended and they should finish up their writing.

Note for Leaders

As your group members share their written reflections for the second time, the hope is that you will hear "I" statements in those reflections. The more comfortable and trusting the group members feel with each other, the more they can risk sharing personal stories—the real juice of this program. It's important that people feel comfortable revealing new facets of their lives to those in the group.

However, as noted in the session plan, the advice contained in "Tips for Giving a Truly Terrible Sermon (50 Ways to Lose Your Listeners)" (Reading E) contradicts this encouragement. Tips #2 and #49 dissuade the preacher from making themselves the star of the show. Invite a conversation about the continuum from self-aggrandizement to meaningful self-disclosure. Remind them, if necessary, that the personal sharing encouraged in this program isn't the shallow "all about me" form but rather using personal experience as a starting point for deeper reflection about larger themes and values.

As this session unfolds, you might notice that some participants are simply unfamiliar with how to speak from their own experience. For example, someone might reflect on a book they read, a chapter from their parents' history, or even current events. These topics are safer than personal sharing, and some participants will need to wade in these waters before they feel ready to dive into uncharted depths.

Generously encourage the participants and offer them pep talks. If necessary, name again—in whatever words are effective—that the spirit of this program is trusting one another as each person takes an inner journey of reflection and processing.

What the Leader Provides

- chalice
- timer
- index cards or paper
- copies of the group's draft covenant

Chalice Pages   15 minutes

Welcome people and, if necessary, remind them that the fifteen minutes of Chalice Pages is spent in silence. Explain that, after this session, the Chalice Pages will be unstructured. For this session, invite them to use some of their fifteen minutes of writing time to create their own prayer or meditation from the template in the session plan by Rev. Lisa Ward, based on Psalm 8. After their meditation is done, they're free to use the rest of the Chalice Pages time to write anything at all.

Tell the group that, when they see you light the chalice, they'll have one minute to finish any stray thoughts and put their pens down. After fourteen minutes, light the chalice.

Reading of Prayers/Meditations   10 minutes

Tell the group that today's session focuses on how to allow creativity and freedom to emerge even within a set of limits. The prayer template they worked with is one example: It might have limited them, but there was still room for their own voices and perspectives.

Invite people to read their prayers or meditations out loud to the group, as they are willing.

Review of Covenant   10 minutes

Invite participants to read the covenant draft (from Session 2) out loud, perhaps taking turns, and then ask whether there's anything the group wants to add or change.

Discussion of Reading C   10 minutes

Lead a discussion of "Can't We Get Along? Loving Your (Political) Opponent" (Reading C), using the questions in the session plan. If participants want to jump ahead to discuss the other homework—the "Do and Don't Tips for Crafting and Leading Worship" and "Tips for Giving a Truly Terrible Sermon (50 Ways to Lose Your Listeners)" readings—gently refocus the discussion; those readings and ideas will be discussed following the break.

Reading and Listening   70 minutes

Invite each person to read their reflection out loud. Ask the group to focus on the questions in the session plan as they listen. After each reflection, honor a minute of silence before the group offers verbal and written feedback to the reader. Ask the listeners to jot some feedback and affirmations on index cards or paper and give them to the reader.

It's likely that as people feel more comfortable listening to reflections, they'll be eager to know more about the person reading. The feedback might turn into questions about the experience itself—for example, if the sermon is about visiting another city, a listener might ask, "Did you visit the art museum when you were there?" or "Don't you have a niece in that city? What's her name?" Since the feedback time is brief and valuable, you may need to redirect these kinds of questions so that tangential conversations can occur during the break or between sessions.

Break   10 minutes

Group Reading: Three Good Guidelines   15 minutes

Read "Three Good Guidelines," found in the session plan, together in silence or out loud, in turns.

Discussion of Group Reading   20 minutes

Lead a discussion of all the tips the group has read about how to preach and not to preach—both in the homework and the group reading—focusing on the questions in the session plan.

Likes and Wishes   5 minutes

Facilitate a discussion in which the group provides both positive and constructive feedback about this session, based on the questions in the session plan.

Review of Preparation for Session 4

As a group, go over the preparation for Session 4, listed in the session plan, Remind the group that, after this session, the program is halfway over (sessions 7 and 8 are reserved for gathering in your worship space to hear full-length sermons). Now is the time for some participants to risk a more personal angle, or to leave behind the book reports to reveal their hearts to the group.

Chalice Pages   15 minutes

Invite the group to write in silence. Extinguish the chalice after fourteen minutes to signal that the session has ended and they should finish up their writing.

What the Leader Provides

- chalice
- timer
- index cards or paper
- copies of the group covenant

Chalice Pages   15 minutes

Welcome people and invite the group to write in silence. After fourteen minutes, light the chalice to signal that they have one minute to finish any stray thoughts and put their pens down.

Reading the Covenant   5 minutes

Take the group's temperature on whether the covenant is serving the group. Invite them to reflect on the questions in the session plan.

Discussion of Reading F   10 minutes

Facilitate a discussion of the reading based on the questions in the session plan. Participants may want to address O'Neill's sermon in terms of whether they liked it, or whether it's "good." If so, gently steer the conversation back to the discussion questions.

Reading and Listening   75 minutes

Invite each person to read their reflection out loud. Ask the group to focus on the questions in the session plan as they listen. After each reflection, honor a minute of silence before the group offers verbal and written feedback to the reader. Ask the listeners to jot down some feedback and affirmations on index cards or paper and give them to the reader.

Break   10 minutes

Reading and Listening   20 minutes

Continue the process of having participants read their reflections while the rest of the group provides written and verbal feedback.

Group Reading: Theological Reflection   25 minutes

Invite participants to read in silence this selection, which is found in the session plan.

Lead a discussion about the reading, focusing on the questions in the session plan.

This is the first time in the program that participants will be exploring the process of theological reflection in depth. If they express concerns about how to do theological reflection, assure them that this session includes a worksheet on page 68 to help them with the process.

Likes and Wishes   5 minutes

Facilitate a discussion in which the group provides both positive and constructive feedback about this session, based on the questions in the session plan.

Review of Preparation for Session 5

As a group, go over the preparation for Session 5, listed in the session plan, and answer any questions.

Chalice Pages   15 minutes

Invite the group to write in silence. After fourteen minutes, extinguish the chalice to signal that the session has ended and they should finish up their writing.

What the Leader Provides

- chalice
- timer
- index cards or paper
- copies of the group covenant

Chalice Pages   15 minutes

Welcome people and invite the group to write in silence. After fourteen minutes, light the chalice to signal that they have one minute to finish any stray thoughts and put their pens down.

Reading the Covenant   5 minutes

By now, the covenant will probably be utterly familiar. Still, remind participants that all are responsible for upholding its promises, and that new promises can be added.

Reading and Listening   60–70 minutes

Invite each person to read their reflection out loud. Ask the group to focus on the questions in the session plan as they listen. After each reflection, honor a minute of silence before the group offers verbal and written feedback to the reader. Ask the listeners to jot some feedback and affirmations on index cards or paper and give them to the reader.

This far into the program, as written reflections lengthen, time management becomes much more complicated—especially if there are more than six participants.

Verbal feedback will have to be curtailed (or perhaps skipped altogether) so that everyone can have the opportunity to read. Since reading out loud is the vehicle for participants' growth and development, make that a priority—even if someone offers to skip their turn reading this time.

Each person was asked to write a reflection of 1,200 words, so each reading should last twelve minutes at most. With one minute of silence to follow and four minutes of feedback for each person, it might take up to seventeen minutes for each person to read and receive feedback. Try to fit in half of your readers before the break. These time limits may seem absurdly precise—but the more you can practice gentle strictness with time, the less likely that your session will run beyond the three-hour mark. Note that the times for reading and listening in this session apply only if all eight participants are present and have prepared reflections of the suggested length. If any participants are absent this day, or come without a written reflection, you can always spend more time discussing theological reflection in the second half of the session.

Break   10 minutes

Reading and Listening   60–70 minutes

Continue the process of having participants read their reflections while the rest of the group provides written and verbal feedback.

Debriefing   5 minutes

Lead a discussion based on the questions in the session plan.

Looking Ahead   5 minutes

Tell the group that in Sessions 7 and 8, they'll deliver full-length sermons (somewhere between 2,000 and 2,200 words, no more than twenty minutes when read at a careful pace). At the next session, they will sign up for the date they prefer.

You might use this time to decide whether to record your final sessions. Video recordings of people delivering their sermons can be helpful, but that decision should be made by the entire group. While video is an effective means of providing feedback, some participants will feel profoundly uncomfortable being recorded, much less watching themselves on video. Also consider that a malfunctioning video camera will take valuable time and attention away from the true purpose of this session, which is to allow participants to feel comfortable in the pulpit as they grow accustomed to the external trappings of preaching.

The same arguments apply to recording sermons with an mp3 recorder. Again, it's up to you as a group to weigh the obvious benefits with the potential disadvantages.

Likes and Wishes   5 minutes

Facilitate a discussion in which the group provides both positive and constructive feedback about this session, based on the questions in the session plan.

Review of Preparation for Session 6

As a group, go over the preparation for Session 6, listed in the session plan, and answer any questions.

Chalice Pages   15 minutes

Invite the group to write in silence. After fourteen minutes, extinguish the chalice to signal that the session has ended and they should finish up their writing.

What the Leader Provides

- chalice
- timer
- index cards or paper
- copies of the group covenant
- sign-up sheet for participants to choose the session (7 or 8) and order in which they'll deliver their sermons

Chalice Pages   10 minutes

Welcome people and let them know that in order to make enough time for reading and responding, this time Chalice Pages will last only ten minutes. Invite the group to write in silence. After nine minutes, light the chalice to signal that they have one minute to finish any stray thoughts and put their pens down.

Reading the Covenant   5 minutes

Go around the circle, taking turns reading the covenant.

Looking Ahead   5 minutes

Remind participants that sessions 7 and 8 will be devoted to hearing full-length sermons. These will be no more than 2,200 words in length for a twenty-minute sermon. If your congregation traditionally has fifteen-minute sermons, participants should write a maximum of 1,700 words. Even if participants have full-length drafts, they probably will not yet consider them complete.

Tell the group that the last two sessions will feel less intimate, and probably less comfortable because of what you'll be doing together. Explain that, one by one, they will stand in the pulpit and read their sermons to the group. This is a significant transition. If up to this point, participants have been unsure of their authority to preach, delivering this sermon might solidify—or rattle—their confidence. Standing in the pulpit means juggling a new and complex set of factors, such as growing comfortable with hearing your voice on the sound system, adapting to the way that light falls on the page, adjusting posture and body language, and finding a natural rhythm of looking back and forth between the manuscript and the congregation.

Go over the suggestions in the session plan for a smooth transition to the pulpit.

Pass around the sign-up sheet so that people can choose the session at which they'll present their sermon. Try to balance the names evenly among the two sessions.

Reading and Listening   65 minutes

At this point, participants will likely have found a comfortable rhythm and depth in the reading process, discovering how to be wise listeners and dispensers of feedback. You can trust them to offer appropriate feedback, but if the group falters, the questions in the previous session plans can serve as guides.

As the leader, you have one last chance to be a gracefully firm timekeeper during this session. As homework, each person was asked to write a reflection of up to 1,500 words—so each reading should last about fifteen minutes, with one minute of silence to follow. Calculate how long each reader will get for both reading and response time if half of your group reflections are heard in the segment before the break. There may not be enough time for verbal feedback, in which case participants will only provide written responses to one another.

Break   5 minutes

Reading and Listening   70 minutes

Continue the process of having participants read their reflections while the rest of the group provides written feedback and, if there is time, verbal feedback as well.

Likes and Wishes   10 minutes

Facilitate a discussion in which the group provides both positive and constructive feedback about this session, based on the questions in the session plan.

You might also plan a celebration—to take place at the end of Session 8 or at a separate time—to formally bring your group to a close.

Review of Preparation for Sessions 7 and 8

As a group, go over the preparation for Sessions 7 and 8, listed in the session plan, and answer any questions.

Chalice Pages   10 minutes

If the reading and listening went over its designated time, use the closing Chalice Pages as an elastic buffer to end on time. Tell participants that this is the last Chalice Pages of the program as there will be no silent writing at sessions 7 and 8.

Invite the group to write in silence. When there is one minute left, extinguish the chalice to signal that the session has ended and they should finish up their writing.

7 and 8

Since your final two sessions will be held in your sanctuary or meeting house, you will need to see to the preparation of that space—whether you prepare it yourself or arrange for it to happen. It's particularly important to arrange—perhaps with the help of your congregation's staff or volunteers—for the sound system to be on and tested before the session begins. Arrive early so that, if necessary, the heat or air-conditioning and lights are also at comfortable levels when the group arrives.

What the Leader Provides

- chalice
- timer
- index cards or paper

Preparing to Listen   15 minutes

Welcome participants and remind them that you will not be writing Chalice Pages. Instead, acknowledge your collective transition into sacred time and space by sitting together in the sanctuary for a few minutes of silence and light the chalice.

Explain the structure of this session: If four people present their sermons, the process of listening and providing feedback, plus a break, should take about two and a half hours. You will time each sermon. Decide during the session's opening, perhaps with the group's input, how it will be handled if someone's sermon goes over the allotted time (fifteen or twenty minutes depending on your congregation's usual practice). Will you ring a bell or say, "Time's up," or will you allow the person to finish their sermon?

Half of the participants (those who signed up for this brave occasion!) will read their sermons. Listeners should scatter themselves throughout the sanctuary, so that they can determine whether the speaker is looking throughout the entire space as they preach, and whether the speaker can be heard in every part of the space. Each sermon will be followed by the usual minute of silence, so that readers can feel what it's like to have their words—and the power of their sermons—remain in the space. (It's recommended that the speaker sit down on the chancel, next to or behind the pulpit, rather than stepping down into the pews during the silence.) Then listeners can gather at the front of the sanctuary, while the speaker remains on the chancel, to offer feedback for ten to fifteen minutes.

Explain that, after each sermon, the group will observe a minute of silence. Ask them to notice what it's like to sit down on the chancel, facing the congregation, when they're done preaching. How do they feel? Some people feel full of adrenaline. Others feel spent. Ask participants to use the silence to be present in their bodies.

Distribute paper and pens for listeners to record their feedback. Remind participants that as speakers, they'll be making significant adjustments to the pulpit. For example, those unaccustomed to speaking in public while standing may unconsciously sway in a distracting manner, or they may falter while reading because the lighting in the sanctuary demands a larger font than the one they used in their manuscript. Listeners may need to provide new forms of gentle feedback.

Preaching and Listening   60 minutes

Half of those preaching today should do so before the break. Following each sermon, observe the minute of silence, then encourage the listeners to applaud.

Break   10 minutes

Preaching and Listening   60 minutes

Continue with the other half of those scheduled to preach today.

Closing   15 minutes

Gather together again in a circle and share silence, a song familiar to the congregation, or a group hug (or all three!).

Ending the Program

When these eight sessions are over, some people find it difficult to allow the group to truly end. Saying good-bye might be hard. You all may have come to rely on the infusion of love and support that the members provide, or wish to continue getting feedback on a not-quite-done sermon. Endings can be difficult.

To provide closure for members of your group, consider celebrating both your relationships and your sermons with a potluck dinner, or some other form of fellowship. If you do hold a social gathering, make sure that you take the time to name what you're grateful for, and what you've learned from your sessions. Encourage the group to praise and thank each other.

As a closing exercise, you might also choose to engage and discuss the Guiding Principles used by the Center for Pastoral Effectiveness, a United Methodist Institute for ministers, provided in the session plan.

When you finally draw the program to a close—when the books are put away, the sessions are over, and the accursed timekeeping responsibilities are just a memory—allow yourself some private moments of satisfaction, gratitude, and growth. Where did you feel confident, as Leader? How did you feel valued? Is there anyone to whom you owe appreciation? What moments of grace or magic did you experience in your leadership role? Did you learn new skills? Is there anything you'd do differently, knowing what you now know?

However smooth or bumpy the program's progression, your willingness to be a facilitator is a gift to those in the group, and by extension to your congregation. Bask in that gladness, when it arrives, and keep serving the people and the faith that you love.

Acknowledgments

My thanks-giving begins with colleagues, named and unnamed in the preceding pages, who lent their wisdom and counsel to this project. I'm continually grateful for the camaraderie of my fellow clergy. You, dear ones, are beloved partners in this humbling, life-giving, sacred work where "still we strive in expectation."

The book you're holding grew out of an a-ha moment, sparked a decade ago by my colleague Grace Simons. I thank her for inspiring me to stumble my way through creating a program for my former parishioners at Live Oak Unitarian Universalist Congregation in Goleta, California. I say "stumble" because it took more than four years to turn my skeleton of vague ideas into a full-blown, reasonably well-oiled system that we at Live Oak called the Summer Sermon Seminar. Shared ministry being what it is, I didn't do it alone.

That the Seminar clicked, let alone blossomed and transformed that congregation, is testament to those who eagerly participated. I'm grateful to the following people— some of whom confided initially that they would "never" get up to preach a sermon, and then did so with tremendous grace and confidence, in some cases more than once:

Lisl, Sue, Liz, Virginia, Drew, Barb, Mary, Ellen, Elaine, Wilson, Melanie, Marty, Pat, Patrick, Kristine, Kathryn, Noa, Barbara, Gloria, Kanta, Fermina, Paul, Kristin, Jim, Lars, Lizzie, Kristen, Jim, Ken, Emily, Jen, and Ela.

As the tender hearts who spent many summer nights bringing your authentic selves and loving presence to one another, you are the co-creators of this book. Thank you.

Also by Erika Hewitt

Story, Song, and Spirit
Fun and Creative Worship Services for All Ages
Skinner House Books, 2010

These multigenerational worship services draw from folk tales, children's literature, and everyday living. Hewitt offers new ways to celebrate the beginning of the church year, Christmas, coming of age, and Earth Day, as well as services for any time, to engage children through elders. Each service is a whole body experience, inviting members to participate and engage the mind, heart, and spirit. These fully scripted services include recommended hymns, readings, and props, plus quick, at-a-glance descriptions that rate each service based on the preparation time required.

"Hewitt understands the need for careful and thorough preparation for worship which also leaves room for the spirit in the moment. Her thorough directions on props, stage directions, transitions, and liturgical elements make all the difference in seeing these stories fully integrated into satisfying and creative worship services for all ages."
—Wayne Arnason, co-author, *Worship That Works*

"Woven together with a strong sense of liturgical rhythm, Hewitt brings together every element that today's multigenerational UU community needs to offer engaged and spirited worship."
—Greg Ward, minister, Unitarian Universalist Church
    of the Monterey Peninsula